The Family Seder

A Traditional Passover Haggadah For the Modern Home

Prepared by

Rabbi Alfred J. Kolatch

Jonathan David Publishers
New York

THE FAMILY SEDER

Copyright © 1967, 1991
by
ALFRED J. KOLATCH

No part of this book may be reproduced in any form
whatsoever without the prior written consent of the publishers.
Address all inquiries to:

Jonathan David Publishers, Inc.
68-22 Eliot Avenue
Middle Village, New York   11379

23 24 25

ISBN 0-8246-0132-7

Printed in the United States of America

Preface

The Family Seder is a traditional Haggadah. It contains the complete Hebrew text.

Historically, not all Haggadahs published throughout the ages were uniform in the order of the service. In *The Family Seder* a few changes have been made in the order of the service because it was felt that this improved the sequence, particularly in the historical sections.

The English rendition is not a literal translation. While based for the most part on the Hebrew text, it enlarges upon it where such additions enhance the meaning.

The main motivation has been to make *The Family Seder* a meaningful and inspirational experience for the modern Jew. As such, even those whose knowledge of Hebrew is limited, and may prefer to skip many of the Hebrew sections, will find that the English portion stands as a complete entity.

Special thanks are due to the following artists whose drawings have been used in this book: Irene Burstein, Lil Goldstein, Naamah Kitov, Eric Ray and Samuel Sigaloff.

ALFRED J. KOLATCH

The Seder Table and Its Symbols

In addition to the normal, elaborate table setting which one would arrange for any festive meal, the following items should be prepared. All need not be placed on the table initially, but they should be prepared before the Seder begins, and kept in readiness.

1. The first important item is the *matzo*. Three whole *matzōs* are required to be set at the head of the table. Specially designed *matzo* bags are available with three compartments, one for each *matzo*. Otherwise, ordinary paper or cloth napkins can be used.

   At regular Sabbath and festival meals only two loaves of bread (*challōs*) are used over which the blessing is recited. In order to distinguish the Passover festival, instead of using just two *matzōs* (as substitutes for the leavened bread which is prohibited on Passover), a third is used to mark the joyous nature of the occasion. Some scholars have interpreted the use of three *matzōs* as representing the whole Jewish community: priests, levites and Israelites.

   The three *matzōs* are usually placed beneath the Seder tray.

1

2. A Seder tray, which is available in many styles, must be prepared in advance, and is placed at the head of the table. This tray usually has six circular indentations in which the most important Passover Seder food-symbols are placed. These symbols are pointed to from time to time in the course of the Seder. They are not to be consumed. The symbolic foods are the following:

a. *Morōr* (Bitter Herbs). Either the head of a horseradish, or bottled, white horseradish is used. The *morōr* symbolizes the bitter lot of the enslaved Israelites described in the Haggadah. Place a small amount of horseradish (white, preferably) in the *morōr* compartment. An extra dish of grated horseradish should be set aside with a sufficient amount for each participant to have a small helping during the Seder.

b. *Karpas* (Vegetable). At one point in the Seder, we dip a vegetable in salt water. This custom was prevalent in ancient times, and is explained more fully in the text. Celery, parsley, cucumber, radish or potato are among the vegetables commonly used. Place a small piece of any of these vegetables in the *karpas* compartment.

c. *Charōses*. This is a mixture of chopped apples, walnuts and cinnamon, moistened with wine. The *charōses* is symbolic of the mortar the Children of Israel were compelled to make for their Egyptian taskmasters. A sufficient amount is prepared for all to have about a half teaspoonful during the Seder. Place a small amount in the appropriate place on the Seder tray.

Heinrich Heine, in his early 19th century novelette, *The Rabbi of Bacherach,* describes the *charōses* prepared in a German household as consisting of raisins, cinnamon and nuts. In the Mishna (Pesachim 10:3), the *charōses* is described as consisting of nuts and fruits, pounded together, and mixed with vinegar.

2

d. *Z'rōa* (Bone). The bone is symbolic of the "mighty arm" of God, as the Bible describes it, which influenced Pharaoh to release the Children of Israel from bondage. In some families a meat bone is roasted, and in others the neck of a chicken or some other fowl is roasted and is used as the symbol for the Seder tray.

e. *Baytzo* (Egg). A hardboiled egg is roasted and placed on the Seder tray. The egg is symbolic of the festival sacrifice brought in Temple days. Some authorities have interpreted it as a symbol of mourning for the loss of the Temple. (The Second Temple was destroyed by the Romans in the year 70 C.E.). The egg is a symbolic food eaten by mourners. Its oval shape (denoting no beginning and no end) symbolizes eternal life. Extra hardboiled eggs (shelled) should be prepared to distribute to each participant later during the Seder.

f. *Chazeres* (Vegetable). Most modern Seder trays have this sixth compartment. *Chazeres* serves a function similar to the *morōr,* mentioned above. The vegetable usually placed in this compartment is lettuce, watercress, radish, or any variety that would have a tendency to be (or become) bitter.

The biblical verse, "They shall eat it (the paschal lamb) with unleavened bread and bitter herbs," (Numbers 9:11) is probably the basis for the use of *chazeres* as one of the symbolic foods. The verse speaks of bitter herbs (plural) and not *a* bitter herb. Therefore, two types of bitter herbs (vegetables that have a bitter tang) were introduced. The Mishna (Pesachim 2:6) speaks of *chazeres* as one of the herbs (vegetables) that can be used on Passover to fulfill one's religious obligation. It was not, however, uniformly adopted by all authorities.

Rabbi Isaac Luria, the 16th century mystic of German extraction, also known as the "Ari" (using the initials: *ha-Ashkenazi Rabbi Isaac*), is known to have used *chazeres* as one of the symbolic foods on his Passover table. But, the equally great 18th century scholar, Rabbi Elijah of Lithuania (better known as "The Vilna Gaon"), did not place *chazeres* on his Seder table.

3. Wine goblets are placed at each setting for each participant, and a decanter of wine is prepared. The wine goblets are to be filled four times in the course of the Seder. At normal Sabbath and festival meals a cup of wine is served for *kiddush,* and another when the aftermeal Grace is recited. But because of the joyous nature of Passover, two additional cups were added. One is consumed after the "story" of the Haggadah is read (which ends before Grace), and the other at the conclusion of the service (just before the hymns and songs).

   Of the many additional explanations offered for this practice of drinking four cups of wine, the most popular is that they are reminders of the four verbs used in the Bible to describe the drama of redemption (Exodus 6:6-7): a) I will *bring* you out from Egypt; b) I will *deliver* you from their bondage; c) I will *redeem* you with an outstretched arm; d) I will *take* you to Me for a people.

   Red wine is commonly used, although there were times in Jewish history (particularly during the Middle Ages) when white wine was used because blood-libel accusations were leveled against Jews, claiming that Jews used the blood of Christian children at the Seder ceremonies.

   Drinking four cups of wine was always considered important. As far back as talmudic times, the view was expressed that even the poorest man in Israel should not drink less than four cups of wine at the Seder.

4. Salt Water. Several saucers or cups with salt water should be placed on the table to be used for the dipping of the vegetable. In Jerusalem of the first and second centuries, it was common practice to dip a vegetable (which was the *hors d'oeuvres* that preceded a meal) in salt water. There is a custom among many people today to place a small dish of salt water or vinegar on the Seder tray, along with the other symbolic foods.

5. A pillow is prepared for the leader to recline against (and in some households each participant uses a pillow). This custom, of eating in a reclining position, is of Persian origin, and symbolizes the life of a free man. Greek and Roman patricians continued this practice, and Jews, who lived in their midst, adopted it as a meaningful expression of a free and unharried life.

6. Elijah's Cup. A special, decorative goblet is placed on the table, which is called the Cup of Elijah. It is filled with wine, along with all others, after the meal is over and the Grace has been recited. Elijah, the great prophet in Israel, who dominated the Palestinian scene 28 centuries ago, and was the conscience of Israel in the days of King Ahab and Queen Jezebel, has become synonymous in Judaism with the Messianic Age. In his lifetime, Elijah fought the forces of paganism, and the Bible pictures his death in miraculous terms. He did not die, but ascended to heaven in a chariot, and vanished. His return was looked forward to, and was to mark the advent of an age of harmony, peace and understanding among all peoples, and all nations.

7. Naturally, a Passover Haggadah should be placed alongside each setting.

8. Before nightfall, the mistress of the house should light the festival candles and, as on any other holiday or Sabbath, should pronounce the appropriate blessings.

The blessings are to be found on the next page.

CANDLE LIGHTING CEREMONY

On Friday evening only
add the words in brackets.

בָּרוּךְ אַתָּה, יְיָ אֱלֹהֵינוּ, מֶלֶךְ
הָעוֹלָם, אֲשֶׁר קִדְּשָׁנוּ בְּמִצְוֹתָיו וְצִוָּנוּ
לְהַדְלִיק נֵר שֶׁל [שַׁבָּת וְשֶׁל] יוֹם טוֹב.

בָּרוּךְ אַתָּה, יְיָ אֱלֹהֵינוּ, מֶלֶךְ
הָעוֹלָם, שֶׁהֶחֱיָנוּ וְקִיְּמָנוּ וְהִגִּיעָנוּ לַזְּמַן
הַזֶּה.

*Boruch ato Adōnoy, Elōhaynu melech
ho-ōlom, asher ki-d'shonu b'mitzvōsov,
v'tzeevonu l'hadlik nayr shel [Shabos
v'shel] yōm tōv.*

Praised art Thou, O Lord our God,
King of the universe, Who hast sanctified
us with Thy commandments, and commanded us to kindle [the Sabbath and]
the festival lights.

*Boruch ato Adōnoy, Elōhaynu melech
ho-ōlom, she-heche-yonu v'kee-monu,
v'heegeeyonu, lazman hazeh.*

Praised art Thou, O Lord our God,
King of the universe, Who hast brought
us life, and sustained us, and enabled us
to reach this season of joy.

All are seated around the table, and the leader, or one of the participants, reads the following introduction:

The Essence of Passover

"Passover has a message for the conscience and the heart of all mankind. For what does it commemorate? It commemorates the deliverance of a people from degrading slavery, from most foul and cruel tyranny. And so, it is Israel's—nay, God's protest against unrighteousness, whether individual or national. Wrong, it declares, may triumph for a time, but even though it be perpetrated by the strong on the weak, it will meet with its inevitable retribution at last."[1]

Although we, who mouth the words and recite the ritual, are reliving an epoch which is peculiar to *Jewish* history, the drama that is Passover is no longer ours alone. Its enactment is not confined only to the dining rooms of our own homes; it has been embraced by the world at large, and is continually being reenacted on the stage of mankind by all who seek avenues to assert their condemnation of oppression and tyranny, by all who labor in the vineyard of the Lord searching for freedom and peace.

Although it is the Pharaoh of old who is the tyrant of the Haggadah, it is not he alone of whom we speak tonight. We speak this evening of other tyrants and other tyrannies as well. We speak

Of the tyranny of poverty
And the tyranny of privation,

Of the tyranny of wealth
And the tyranny of war,

Of the tyranny of power
And the tyranny of despair,

Of the tyranny of disease
And the tyranny of time,

Of the tyranny of ignorance
And the tyranny of color.

---

[1] Morris Joseph: *Judaism As Creed and Life.*

To all these tyrannies do we address ourselves this evening. Passover brands them all as abominations in the sight of God.

With Thomas Jefferson we say: "I have sworn upon the altar of God, eternal hostility against every form of tyranny over the mind."

And with Abraham Lincoln we affirm: "As I would not be a *slave,* so I would not be a *master.* This expresses my idea of democracy. Whatever differs from this, to the extent of the difference, is no democracy."

The spirit of Passover, although created of the flesh and sinew of Judaism, belongs to all mankind. "Since the Exodus," said Heinrich Heine, "freedom has spoken with a Hebrew accent." Today it speaks in the language of all men.

Opening Prayer

O Lord, our God:

We have gathered on this festive evening, at this Seder table, to recall, retell and re-enact the early history of our people who, from biblical days onward, were infused with a burning desire to achieve freedom.

We pray, as we sit here assembled in family friendship, and as we relive in words and symbols the ancient quest for liberty, that we shall become infused with renewed spirit and inspiration and understanding. May the problem of all who are down-trodden be our problem; may the concern of all who are afflicted be our concern; and may the struggle of all who strive for liberty and equality be our struggle.

In this spirit, we now raise our cups to sanctify Thy Name in the words of the ancient *kiddush,* which emphasizes our thankfulness for this holiday of *Pesach,* the Festival of Freedom, marking the Exodus from Egypt.

"Be not forgetful of prayer. Every time you pray, if your prayer is sincere, there will be a new feeling and new meaning in it, which will give you fresh courage, and you will understand that prayer is an education."

FYODOR DOSTOYEVSKY

Sanctification (Kiddush)

The first of the four cups of wine is now poured, and the leader, together with participants, recites the *kiddush.* (The *kiddush,* or prayer of sanctification, is recited before all Sabbath and festival meals.) Words in parentheses are recited if the Seder is held on a Friday night.

Recite this paragraph on Friday night only:

וַיְהִי־עֶרֶב וַיְהִי־בֹקֶר

יוֹם הַשִּׁשִּׁי. וַיְכֻלּוּ הַשָּׁמַיִם וְהָאָרֶץ וְכָל צְבָאָם. וַיְכַל אֱלֹהִים בַּיּוֹם הַשְּׁבִיעִי מְלַאכְתּוֹ אֲשֶׁר עָשָׂה. וַיִּשְׁבֹּת בַּיּוֹם הַשְּׁבִיעִי מִכָּל מְלַאכְתּוֹ אֲשֶׁר עָשָׂה. וַיְבָרֶךְ אֱלֹהִים אֶת־יוֹם הַשְּׁבִיעִי וַיְקַדֵּשׁ אֹתוֹ כִּי בוֹ שָׁבַת מִכָּל מְלַאכְתּוֹ אֲשֶׁר בָּרָא אֱלֹהִים לַעֲשׂוֹת.

Yōm ha-shee-shee, va-y'chulu ha-shoma-yim v'ho-oretz v'chol tz'vo-om. Va-y'chal Elōhim ba-yōm ha-sh'vee-ee m'lachtō asher oso. Va-yishbōs ba-yōm ha-sh'vee-ee mee-kol m'lachtō asher oso. Va-y'vorech Elōhim es yōm ha-sh'vee-ee va-y'kadaysh ōsō, kee vō sho-vas mee-kol m'lachtō asher boro Elōhim la-asōs.

The heavens and the earth were created, and all that was in them. And on the seventh day God finished His work, and rested. And God blessed the seventh day and declared it holy, for on it He rested from all His work of creation.

On weekdays begin here:

בָּרוּךְ אַתָּה יְיָ, אֱלֹהֵינוּ מֶלֶךְ הָעוֹלָם, בּוֹרֵא, פְּרִי הַגָּפֶן.

Boruch ato Adōnoy, Elōhaynu melech ho-ōlom,
bōray pree ha- gofen.

Praised be Thou, O Lord our God, King of the universe,
Who createst the fruit of the vine.

10

רוּךְ אַתָּה יְיָ, אֱלֹהֵינוּ מֶלֶךְ הָעוֹלָם, אֲשֶׁר
בָּחַר בָּנוּ מִכָּל־עָם, וְרוֹמְמָנוּ מִכָּל־לָשׁוֹן,
וְקִדְּשָׁנוּ בְּמִצְוֹתָיו, וַתִּתֶּן־לָנוּ יְיָ אֱלֹהֵינוּ בְּאַהֲבָה
(שַׁבָּתוֹת לִמְנוּחָה וּ) מוֹעֲדִים לְשִׂמְחָה, חַגִּים
וּזְמַנִּים לְשָׂשׂוֹן, אֶת יוֹם (הַשַּׁבָּת הַזֶּה, וְאֶת יוֹם)
חַג הַמַּצּוֹת הַזֶּה. זְמַן חֵרוּתֵנוּ (בְּאַהֲבָה) מִקְרָא
קֹדֶשׁ, זֵכֶר לִיצִיאַת מִצְרָיִם. כִּי בָנוּ בָחַרְתָּ,
וְאוֹתָנוּ קִדַּשְׁתָּ, מִכָּל־הָעַמִּים. (וְשַׁבָּת וּ) מוֹעֲדֵי
קָדְשְׁךָ (בְּאַהֲבָה וּבְרָצוֹן) בְּשִׂמְחָה וּבְשָׂשׂוֹן
הִנְחַלְתָּנוּ. בָּרוּךְ אַתָּה יְיָ, מְקַדֵּשׁ (הַשַּׁבָּת
וְ) יִשְׂרָאֵל וְהַזְּמַנִּים.

*Boruch ato Adōnoy Elōhaynu melech ho-ōlom asher bochar bonu
meekol om, v'rō-memonu meekol loshōn, v'kideshonu b'mitzvōsov.
Va-teetayn lonu Adōnoy Elōhaynu b'ahavo (Shabosōs lim'nucho
u-) mō-adim l'simcho, chagim u-z'manim l'sosōn, es yōm (ha-
Shabos hazeh, v'es yōm) chag hamatzōs hazeh. Z'man chayrusaynu
(b'ahavo) mikro kōdesh, zaycher lee-tzee-as Mitzro-yim. Kee
vonu vo-charto, v'ōsonu kee-dash-to meekol ho-amim, (V'shab-
bos) Umō-aday kodshecho (b'a-ha-vo u'v'rotzōn) hin-chal-tonu.
Boruch ato Adōnoy, m'kadaysh (ha-shabos v') yisroayl v'haze-
manim.*

Praised be Thou, O Lord, our God, King of the universe, Who
hast chosen us from among all nations, and hast exalted us above
all peoples, and hast sanctified us through Thy commandments.
With great love hast Thou bequeathed unto us (Sabbaths for peace
and) festivals for joyfulness. Thou hast bestowed upon us (this
Sabbath day and) this Festival of Matzos, as a day of freedom, in
commemoration of the Exodus from Egypt.

11

On Saturday night only, add:

בָּרוּךְ אַתָּה יְיָ אֱלֹהֵינוּ מֶלֶךְ הָעוֹלָם. בּוֹרֵא מְאוֹרֵי הָאֵשׁ.

בָּרוּךְ אַתָּה יְיָ אֱלֹהֵינוּ מֶלֶךְ הָעוֹלָם. הַמַּבְדִּיל בֵּין קֹדֶשׁ לְחוֹל.
בֵּין אוֹר לְחֹשֶׁךְ. בֵּין יִשְׂרָאֵל לָעַמִּים. בֵּין יוֹם הַשְּׁבִיעִי לְשֵׁשֶׁת יְמֵי
הַמַּעֲשֶׂה. בֵּין קְדֻשַּׁת שַׁבָּת לִקְדֻשַּׁת יוֹם טוֹב הִבְדַּלְתָּ וְאֶת יוֹם
הַשְּׁבִיעִי מִשֵּׁשֶׁת יְמֵי הַמַּעֲשֶׂה קִדַּשְׁתָּ. הִבְדַּלְתָּ וְקִדַּשְׁתָּ אֶת עַמְּךָ יִשְׂרָאֵל
בִּקְדֻשָּׁתֶךָ. בָּרוּךְ אַתָּה יְיָ הַמַּבְדִּיל בֵּין קֹדֶשׁ לְקֹדֶשׁ.

Boruch ato Adōnoy Elōhaynu melech ho-ōlom, bōray m'ōray ho-aysh.

Boruch ato Adōnoy Elōhaynu melech ho-ōlom, hamavdil bayn kōdesh l'chōl, bayn ōr l'chōshech, bayn Yisroyal lo-amim, bayn yōm ha-sh'vee-ee l'shayshes y'may ha-maaseh; bayn k'dushas Shabos lik'dushas yōm tōv hivdalto, v'es yom ha-sh'vee-ee mee-shayshes y'may ha-maaseh keedashto; hivdalto v'keedashto es am'cho Yisroayl bikdushosecho. Boruch ato Adōnoy, hamavdil bayn kōdesh l'kōdesh.

Praised be Thou, O Lord our God, King of the universe, Who created the heavenly luminaries.

Praised be Thou, O Lord our God, King of the universe, Who distinguishes between the sacred and secular, between light and darkness, between Israel and other peoples, and between the seventh day of rest and the six days of labor. Blessed art Thou, O Lord our God, Who differentiates between the holiness of the Sabbath and the holiness of the festival.

"America has believed that in differentiation, not in uniformity, lies the path of progress."   LOUIS D. BRANDEIS

12

At every Seder service add:

בָּרוּךְ אַתָּה יְיָ, אֱלֹהֵינוּ מֶלֶךְ הָעוֹלָם,
שֶׁהֶחֱיָנוּ, וְקִיְּמָנוּ, וְהִגִּיעָנוּ, לַזְּמַן הַזֶּה.

Boruch ato Adōnoy Elōhaynu melech ho-ōlom, she-he-cheyonu,
v'keemonu, v'hee-geeyonu la-z'man ha-zeh.

Praised be Thou, O Lord our God, who hast kept us in life,
and has sustained us, and permitted us to enjoy this festive day.

All participants are seated and drink first cup of wine.

Washing the Hands

According to an ancient practice, recorded in the Talmud, the
hands are to be washed before food is dipped into a liquid (or
sauce), which is the next ceremony in the Seder ritual. Although
this practice has fallen into general disuse, it has been kept as
part of the Seder. A pitcher of water (with a bowl and a towel)
is taken around the table by the mistress of the house, and water
is poured on the hands of each participant. In some families the
participants leave the table to wash at a sink. No blessing is
recited at this point, since a full meal is not to be eaten now.

Hors D'Oeuvres (Karpas)

A piece of *karpas* (vegetable) is now distributed to all participants. The vegetable used varies in different households. It may
be cucumber, lettuce, radish, parsley, potato, or any other
type. Each participant dips his vegetable in a dish of salt water,
and then all recite the blessing in unison. In Jerusalem of the
first and second centuries, it was common practice to begin a
formal meal by passing around *hors d'oeuvres* which usually
consisted of a vegetable dipped in salt water.

בָּרוּךְ אַתָּה יְיָ, אֱלֹהֵינוּ מֶלֶךְ הָעוֹלָם,
בּוֹרֵא פְּרִי הָאֲדָמָה.

13

Boruch ato Adōnoy, Elōhaynu melech ho-ōlom, bōray pree ho-adomo.

Praised be Thou, O Lord our God, King of the universe, Who is the Creator of the fruit of the earth.

Breaking the Matzo

The leader now takes the middle *matzo* from the set of three, and breaks it in half. He replaces one half, and then places the second half in a napkin or bag, setting it aside, to be distributed as the *afikomon* (dessert) at the end of the meal. This custom of setting aside half of the *matzo* was unknown before the 13th century. It has since become an exciting part of the Seder ceremonies for the children would "steal" the *afikomon* and hide it from the leader. The Seder service cannot be continued until the leader finds it, or offers the children a gift for its recovery.

Reciting the Haggadah

The leader uncovers the top *matzo*, exposing it slightly. He then raises the tray or container holding the *matzos,* and all join in reciting the following:

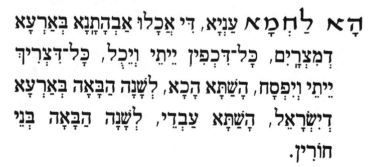

הָא לַחְמָא עַנְיָא, דִּי אֲכָלוּ אַבְהָתָנָא בְּאַרְעָא דְמִצְרָיִם, כָּל־דִּכְפִין יֵיתֵי וְיֵכֻל, כָּל־דִּצְרִיךְ יֵיתֵי וְיִפְסַח, הָשַׁתָּא הָכָא, לְשָׁנָה הַבָּאָה בְּאַרְעָא דְיִשְׂרָאֵל, הָשַׁתָּא עַבְדֵי, לְשָׁנָה הַבָּאָה בְּנֵי חוֹרִין.

THE SYMBOL OF AFFLICTION

Ho lachmo anyo dee-acholu avosono b'aro d'mitzro-yim. Kol dichfin yaysay v'yay-chōl; kol ditzrich yaysay v'yifsach. Ho-shato hocho; l'shono ha-bo-o b'aro d'Yisroayl. Ho-shato avday; l'shono ha-bo-o b'nay chōrin.

Behold this *matzo*—the symbol of affliction and poverty. It is the bread that our ancestors ate as slaves in the land of Egypt. We are mindful tonight of the hardships they suffered and the cruelty they endured. To all who are in need we therefore say: We know your suffering, and we are anxious to help you in your need. To all who are hungry we say: Come and join us in our abundance. Let it be known to all men that, because of our history, we understand the plight of the poor; we know what it is to suffer. We pray *with* them, and *for* them, that the coming year will bring with it the promise of a better life.

"No man can be perfectly free until *all* are free; no one can be perfectly moral till *all* are moral; no one can be perfectly happy till *all* are happy."

HERBERT SPENCER

"A hungry man is not a free man."

ADLAI STEVENSON

The leader covers the *matzo* and replaces the tray. The wine cup of each participant is filled. Then, the youngest one present recites the four questions which expresses his sense of wonder over the unusual customs and different foods eaten on this festive occasion. The significance of the foods and symbols referred to is explained in the introductory section, "The Seder Table and Its Symbols."

The Four Questions

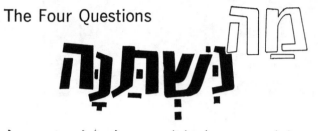

מַה נִּשְׁתַּנָּה הַלַּיְלָה הַזֶּה מִכָּל הַלֵּילוֹת. שֶׁבְּכָל הַלֵּילוֹת אָנוּ אוֹכְלִין חָמֵץ וּמַצָּה. הַלַּיְלָה הַזֶּה כֻּלּוֹ מַצָּה.

שֶׁבְּכָל הַלֵּילוֹת אָנוּ אוֹכְלִין שְׁאָר יְרָקוֹת. הַלַּיְלָה הַזֶּה מָרוֹר.

שֶׁבְּכָל הַלֵּילוֹת אֵין אָנוּ מַטְבִּילִין אֲפִילוּ פַּעַם אֶחָת. הַלַּיְלָה הַזֶּה שְׁתֵּי פְעָמִים.

שֶׁבְּכָל הַלֵּילוֹת אָנוּ אוֹכְלִין בֵּין יוֹשְׁבִין וּבֵין מְסֻבִּין. הַלַּיְלָה הַזֶּה כֻּלָּנוּ מְסֻבִּין.

16

The Four Questions

Youngest: Ma nishtano ha-lailo ha-zeh meekol ha-laylōs?
Why is this night different from all other nights?

Leader: In what way do you find this night different?

Youngest: In four ways do I find it different.

Leader: What is the first difference?

Youngest: She-b'chol ha-laylōs onu ōchlin chomaytz u-matzo, ha-lailo ha-zeh kulō matzo.
It differs in that on all other nights we eat bread or *matzo,* while on this night we eat only *matzo.*

Leader: And what is the second difference?

Youngest: She-b'chol ha-laylōs onu ōchlin sh'or y'rokōs, ha-lailo ha-zeh morōr.
It differs in that on all other nights we eat vegetables and herbs of all kinds, while on this night we must eat bitter herbs.

Leader: And what is the third difference between this night and all other nights?

Youngest: She-b'chol ha-laylōs ayn onu matbeelin afeelu paam echos, ha-lailo ha-zeh shtay f'omim.
It differs in that on all other nights we do not dip vegetables even once, while on this night we dip them twice.

Leader: And what is the fourth difference?

Youngest: She-b'chol ha-laylōs onu ōchlin bayn yōshvin u-vayn m'subin, ha-lailo ha-zeh kulonu m'subin.
It differs in that on all other nights we eat in an upright or a reclining position, while on this night we recline at the table.

Leader:

You have asked four important questions that involve four unusual practices and ceremonies that take place at the Passover Seder table. To find the answer we must go back to the early history of our people, to the days of Moses and Aaron who were trying to raise the hopes of their fellow Israelites, crushed and beaten by a merciless tyrant.

Slaves Were We

עֲבָדִים הָיִינוּ לְפַרְעֹה בְּמִצְרָיִם, וַיּוֹצִיאֵנוּ יְיָ אֱלֹהֵינוּ מִשָּׁם, בְּיָד חֲזָקָה וּבִזְרוֹעַ נְטוּיָה, וְאִלּוּ לֹא הוֹצִיא, הַקָּדוֹשׁ בָּרוּךְ הוּא, אֶת־אֲבוֹתֵינוּ מִמִּצְרַיִם, הֲרֵי אָנוּ, וּבָנֵינוּ וּבְנֵי בָנֵינוּ, מְשֻׁעְבָּדִים הָיִינוּ לְפַרְעֹה בְּמִצְרָיִם, וַאֲפִלּוּ כֻּלָּנוּ חֲכָמִים, כֻּלָּנוּ נְבוֹנִים, כֻּלָּנוּ זְקֵנִים, כֻּלָּנוּ יוֹדְעִים אֶת־הַתּוֹרָה, מִצְוָה עָלֵינוּ לְסַפֵּר בִּיצִיאַת מִצְרָיִם. וְכָל־הַמַּרְבֶּה לְסַפֵּר בִּיצִיאַת מִצְרַיִם הֲרֵי זֶה מְשֻׁבָּח.

Assembly:

We were once slaves to the Pharaoh of Egypt, and God in all His glory and power, caused the shackles of slavery to be broken. He redeemed us, and brought us forth into freedom. And had this great miracle of history not been bestowed upon us, we, to this day, and our children after us, might still be subjects of the Pharaohs of Egypt. We, therefore, consider it a sacred duty and obligation to keep this miracle of salvation ever alive in our memories. And it matters not how wise or learned we are, or how well versed we are in the teachings of the Torah. The duty of retelling the story of our deliverance from slavery is important and compelling, and must be retold each year at this time. And the more we repeat the story, and dwell upon its message of freedom, the more praiseworthy are we.

"If a nation expects to be ignorant and free, in a state of civilization, it expects what never was and never will be."

THOMAS JEFFERSON

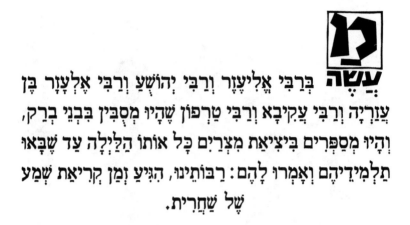

מַ**עֲשֶׂה** בְּרַבִּי אֱלִיעֶזֶר וְרַבִּי יְהוֹשֻׁעַ וְרַבִּי אֶלְעָזָר בֶּן
עֲזַרְיָה וְרַבִּי עֲקִיבָא וְרַבִּי טַרפוֹן שֶׁהָיוּ מְסֻבִּין בִּבְנֵי בְרַק,
וְהָיוּ מְסַפְּרִים בִּיצִיאַת מִצְרַיִם כָּל אוֹתוֹ הַלַּיְלָה עַד שֶׁבָּאוּ
תַלְמִידֵיהֶם וְאָמְרוּ לָהֶם: רַבּוֹתֵינוּ, הִגִּיעַ זְמַן קְרִיאַת שְׁמַע
שֶׁל שַׁחֲרִית.

Leader:

Such was the practice of Jews throughout history. They retold,
reenacted, analyzed and studied the story of the Exodus, always
finding new meaning in it.

Long ago, during the first century, five great scholars and sages,
of both noble and humble backgrounds, sat around the Seder
table at B'nai Berak one Passover eve, and read the words of the
Haggadah, deliberating over their meaning. The Romans had destroyed the Temple and were ruling Palestine with the arm of a
tyrant, reminiscent of the bondage of Egypt. And although it was
in violation of Roman decree to study or teach, there they sat—
these great scholars—unmindful of the hours that were flying by.

A participant continues:

Rabbi Eliezer ben Hyrcanus, the venerated scholar, was there.
In his youth he had bathed in the luxury of his wealthy father's
estate, but, then, despite his father's protestations, the desire to
study grew on him, and he left his comfortable home, and made
his way to the academies of learning in Jerusalem.

A second participant continues:

Next to him sat Rabbi Joshua ben Hananiah, the most unattractive of men, and one of the poorest. He had eked out a pitiful livelihood as a needle-maker. Despite the mockery vented upon him, he was cheerful and tolerant of all people. Unlike Rabbi Eliezer who was militant in his opposition to Rome, Joshua was a pacifist who despised the use of arms.

A third participant continues:

Rabbi Elazar ben Azariah was seated next to Joshua. The son of a wealthy family, and wealthy in his own right, he had achieved fame as a scholar before he turned twenty. He was respected even by the Romans, having visited Rome as a member of a Jewish delegation, but despite his prominence in the community, and despite his noble lineage which he was able to trace back to Ezra the Scribe, he was ever humble.

A fourth participant continues:

Rabbi Akiba ben Joseph sat next to Elazar. Akiba, the self-made scholar, who couldn't read a word until his fortieth birthday! Akiba, the shepherd boy who became the leading light of his generation, supported the efforts of Bar Kochba in his rebellion against Rome. He dared to defy the Roman decree to desist from teaching and, as a result, suffered a violent martyr's death in the year 135.

A fifth participant continues:

And next to Akiba was his former teacher, Rabbi Tarfon. Tarfon the man of great wit and great wealth who could be both vitriolic and gentle! A descendant of a priestly family, he had in his youth participated in the Temple Service. He had little patience with Jews whose loyalty to their faith waivered, but he was very understanding of the human frailties of man and the sacredness of his personality.

Leader:

Each of the five, drawn from different backgrounds, and molded by unequal circumstances, sat and debated the issues of freedom and tyranny the night through, drawing inspiration from the passages of the Haggadah.

Dawn was approaching, and their students, arriving to recite the morning prayers, were stunned by the scene they were witnessing. Five of the greatest scholars locked in discussion and debate the night through!

"Masters!" cried the students, "It is now time to recite the *Shema* of the morning service!"

The *Shema* prayer recited daily, every morning and evening, affirms the traditional Jewish belief in the unity, the oneness, of God to whom undivided loyalty is due. Idolatry, or the multiplicity of gods, by its very nature implies a fragmentation of life, and as such contradicts the notion of One God. The idolatries of today, which include racism, imperialism and totalitarianism are foreign to Judaism, for they express the very antithesis of the *Shema* idea. The denial of any of the rights of the individual, which would tend to obstruct his efforts toward self-fulfillment and self-realization, are a denial of the ideal of God's unity as expressed in the *Shema*.

אָמַר רַבִּי אֶלְעָזָר בֶּן־עֲזַרְיָה. הֲרֵי אֲנִי כְּבֶן־שִׁבְעִים שָׁנָה וְלֹא זָכִיתִי שֶׁתֵּאָמֵר יְצִיאַת מִצְרַיִם בַּלֵּילוֹת. עַד שֶׁדְּרָשָׁהּ בֶּן־זוֹמָא. שֶׁנֶּאֱמַר: לְמַעַן תִּזְכֹּר אֶת־יוֹם צֵאתְךָ מֵאֶרֶץ מִצְרַיִם כֹּל יְמֵי חַיֶּיךָ. יְמֵי חַיֶּיךָ הַיָּמִים. כֹּל יְמֵי חַיֶּיךָ הַלֵּילוֹת. וַחֲכָמִים אוֹמְרִים יְמֵי חַיֶּיךָ הָעוֹלָם הַזֶּה. כֹּל יְמֵי חַיֶּיךָ לְהָבִיא לִימוֹת הַמָּשִׁיחַ.

בָּרוּךְ הַמָּקוֹם, בָּרוּךְ הוּא. בָּרוּךְ שֶׁנָּתַן תּוֹרָה לְעַמּוֹ יִשְׂרָאֵל, בָּרוּךְ הוּא. כְּנֶגֶד אַרְבָּעָה בָנִים דִּבְּרָה תּוֹרָה. אֶחָד חָכָם, וְאֶחָד רָשָׁע, וְאֶחָד תָּם, וְאֶחָד שֶׁאֵינוֹ יוֹדֵעַ לִשְׁאוֹל.

Another participant continues:

The Torah, for which we utter prayers of thanks, is the finest treasure bequeathed unto us by our ancestors of old, for it recognizes this profound truth about freedom.

The surge of freedom does not propel each of us with equal force. Not all see its urgency with the same alacrity. Not all see its immediacy with the same sensitivity. Therefore, to each we must speak on his own level; the questions and doubts of each must be treated individually.

And because not all individuals are alike, and not all nations are alike; because not all can understand or grasp the nuances of Passover alike, and can fathom the full meaning of the freedom of which it speaks, it is imperative that the message be taught repeatedly. Above all, it is the sacred duty of every parent to teach it to his child.

"All we have of freedom, all we use
or know—
This our fathers bought for us
long and long ago."

RUDYARD KIPLING

Another participant continues:

The Torah speaks of four sons, four children, four types of people who must be taught the message of freedom in different ways. Not all are equally equipped to receive its message; not all are equally responsive to its importance; not all can understand the significance of the ritual.

The Four Sons

The Wise Son

חָכָם מַה הוּא אוֹמֵר. מָה הָעֵדֹת וְהַחֻקִּים וְהַמִּשְׁפָּטִים אֲשֶׁר צִוָּה יְיָ אֱלֹהֵינוּ אֶתְכֶם. וְאַף אַתָּה אֱמוֹר לוֹ כְּהִלְכוֹת הַפֶּסַח. אֵין מַפְטִירִין אַחַר הַפֶּסַח אֲפִיקוֹמָן.

Chochom ma hu ōmayr?

The first son is the *chochom,* the wise son.

How does he ask his question about the meaning of Passover? He asks: What is the meaning of all these laws and ordinances that we have been commanded in the Torah? What is their importance?

He is keenly interested in understanding why we observe and how we observe. He wants to follow the law and ceremony, but also wants to understand their significance.

We answer him, by teaching him fully, all that there is to know from beginning to end, from the first ordinance to the last.

The Wicked Son

רָשָׁע מַה הוּא אוֹמֵר. מָה הָעֲבוֹדָה הַזֹּאת לָכֶם. לָכֶם וְלֹא לוֹ. וּלְפִי שֶׁהוֹצִיא אֶת עַצְמוֹ מִן הַכְּלָל וְכָפַר בָּעִקָּר. אַף אַתָּה הַקְהֵה אֶת שִׁנָּיו וֶאֱמוֹר לוֹ. בַּעֲבוּר זֶה עָשָׂה יְיָ לִי בְּצֵאתִי מִמִּצְרָיִם. לִי וְלֹא לוֹ. אִלּוּ הָיָה שָׁם לֹא הָיָה נִגְאָל.

Rosho ma hu ōmayr?

The second son is the *rosho,* the wicked son.

How does the wicked son ask his question? He says: What is the meaning of this Passover service which God commanded *you?* "You," he says, and not "us." By so framing the question he has withdrawn himself from the group, and seems even to deny God.

The wicked son must be answered forthrightly, even sharply. Answer him by quoting the verse: "It is because of that which the Lord did for *me* when I came forth from Egypt." The Exodus from Egypt was a personal triumph for every individual. Feeling the way he does, there is no doubt that the wicked son would not have been liberated from Egypt, had he lived in those wonderful days of redemption.

The Simple Son

תָּם מַה הוּא אוֹמֵר. מַה־זֹּאת. וְאָמַרְתָּ אֵלָיו. בְּחֹזֶק יָד הוֹצִיאָנוּ יְיָ מִמִּצְרַיִם מִבֵּית עֲבָדִים.

Tom ma hu ōmayr?

The third son is the *tom,* the simple son.

How does he put the question about Passover? He asks, very simply: *Ma zōs,* what is this? What is this all about? The events are so overwhelming they confuse and baffle him.

Such a son requires a direct, simple answer that will impress him immediately. Answer him and say simply: "The Passover commemorates and proves the power of God, who brought us out of the land of Egypt, from the house of bondage."

The Naive Son

וְשֶׁאֵינוֹ יוֹדֵעַ לִשְׁאוֹל אַתְּ פְּתַח לוֹ. שֶׁנֶּאֱמַר: וְהִגַּדְתָּ לְבִנְךָ בַּיּוֹם הַהוּא לֵאמֹר. בַּעֲבוּר זֶה עָשָׂה יְיָ לִי בְּצֵאתִי מִמִּצְרָיִם.

V'she-aynō yō-day-a lish-ōl.

The fourth son is naïve—he hardly knows how to ask a question.

This son requires tenderness and assistance in order to arrive at maturity. Assist him by offering to answer the question, which is surely in his mind, but which he is unable to articulate. Say to him: "This holiday of freedom is being celebrated by each of us because of that which the Lord did for *me* when *I* came forth out of Egypt."

יָכוֹל מֵרֹאשׁ חֹדֶשׁ. תַּלְמוּד לוֹמַר בַּיּוֹם הַהוּא. אִי בַּיּוֹם הַהוּא
יָכוֹל מִבְּעוֹד יוֹם. תַּלְמוּד לוֹמַר בַּעֲבוּר זֶה. בַּעֲבוּר זֶה לֹא אָמַרְתִּי
אֶלָּא בְּשָׁעָה שֶׁיֵּשׁ מַצָּה וּמָרוֹר מֻנָּחִים לְפָנֶיךָ.

בָּרוּךְ שׁוֹמֵר הַבְטָחָתוֹ לְיִשְׂרָאֵל. בָּרוּךְ הוּא. שֶׁהַקָּדוֹשׁ בָּרוּךְ הוּא
חִשֵּׁב אֶת הַקֵּץ לַעֲשׂוֹת כְּמָה שֶׁאָמַר לְאַבְרָהָם אָבִינוּ בִּבְרִית בֵּין
הַבְּתָרִים. שֶׁנֶּאֱמַר: וַיֹּאמֶר לְאַבְרָם יָדֹעַ תֵּדַע כִּי גֵר יִהְיֶה זַרְעֲךָ בְּאֶרֶץ
לֹא לָהֶם וַעֲבָדוּם וְעִנּוּ אֹתָם אַרְבַּע מֵאוֹת שָׁנָה. וְגַם אֶת הַגּוֹי אֲשֶׁר
יַעֲבֹדוּ דָּן אָנֹכִי. וְאַחֲרֵי כֵן יֵצְאוּ בִּרְכֻשׁ גָּדוֹל.

Participants raise their cups and recite or sing in unison:

וְהִיא שֶׁעָמְדָה לַאֲבוֹתֵינוּ וְלָנוּ. שֶׁלֹּא אֶחָד
בִּלְבַד, עָמַד עָלֵינוּ לְכַלּוֹתֵנוּ. אֶלָּא שֶׁבְּכָל־דּוֹר
וָדוֹר, עוֹמְדִים עָלֵינוּ לְכַלּוֹתֵנוּ. וְהַקָּדוֹשׁ בָּרוּךְ
הוּא מַצִּילֵנוּ מִיָּדָם.

Recite in unison:

Every generation is duty bound to relive the exodus from Egypt.

The struggle for freedom in Egypt, and the challenge it repre-
sented to our forefathers, is no less the challenge of our age. It is
an ever recurring theme of history.

Freedom is like a reservoir of water that loses its contents with
time, unless it is continuously replenished with fresh water.

AND THOU SHALT TEACH THY CHILDREN ON THAT DAY . . .

Every generation that inherits the victories of the past will not enjoy them unless it strives to understand, appreciate and cherish them as though they themselves had fought for them. Each generation must discover freedom anew; each must ever *earn* its claim to liberty.

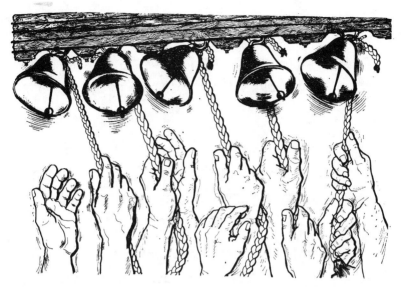

AND THOU SHALT PROCLAIM LIBERTY THROUGHOUT THE LAND!

THE STORY OF PASSOVER

מִתְּחִלָּה עוֹבְדֵי עֲבוֹדָה זָרָה הָיוּ אֲבוֹתֵינוּ. וְעַכְשָׁו קֵרְבָנוּ הַמָּקוֹם
לַעֲבוֹדָתוֹ. שֶׁנֶּאֱמַר: וַיֹּאמֶר יְהוֹשֻׁעַ אֶל־כָּל־הָעָם. כֹּה אָמַר יְיָ אֱלֹהֵי
יִשְׂרָאֵל בְּעֵבֶר הַנָּהָר יָשְׁבוּ אֲבוֹתֵיכֶם מֵעוֹלָם. תֶּרַח אֲבִי אַבְרָהָם
וַאֲבִי נָחוֹר וַיַּעַבְדוּ אֱלֹהִים אֲחֵרִים. וָאֶקַּח אֶת־אֲבִיכֶם אֶת־אַבְרָהָם
מֵעֵבֶר הַנָּהָר. וָאוֹלֵךְ אוֹתוֹ בְּכָל־אֶרֶץ כְּנָעַן וָאַרְבֶּה אֶת־זַרְעוֹ וָאֶתֶּן־לוֹ
אֶת־יִצְחָק. וָאֶתֵּן לְיִצְחָק אֶת־יַעֲקֹב וְאֶת־עֵשָׂו. וָאֶתֵּן לְעֵשָׂו אֶת־הַר שֵׂעִיר
לָרֶשֶׁת אוֹתוֹ וְיַעֲקֹב וּבָנָיו יָרְדוּ מִצְרָיִם.

"People will not look forward to posterity who never look backward to
their ancestors."

EDMUND BURKE

29

אַ וּלְמַד מַה־בִּקֵּשׁ לָבָן הָאֲרַמִּי לַעֲשׂוֹת לְיַעֲקֹב אָבִינוּ. שֶׁפַּרְעֹה
לֹא גָזַר אֶלָּא עַל־הַזְּכָרִים וְלָבָן בִּקֵּשׁ לַעֲקוֹר אֶת־הַכֹּל. שֶׁנֶּאֱמַר:
אֲרַמִּי אֹבֵד אָבִי וַיֵּרֶד מִצְרַיְמָה וַיָּגָר שָׁם בִּמְתֵי מְעָט וַיְהִי־שָׁם לְגוֹי גָּדוֹל
עָצוּם וָרָב.

וַיֵּרֶד מִצְרַיְמָה. אָנוּס עַל־פִּי הַדִּבּוּר: וַיָּגָר שָׁם. מְלַמֵּד שֶׁלֹּא יָרַד
לְהִשְׁתַּקֵּעַ בְּמִצְרַיִם אֶלָּא לָגוּר שָׁם. שֶׁנֶּאֱמַר: וַיֹּאמְרוּ אֶל־פַּרְעֹה לָגוּר
בָּאָרֶץ בָּאנוּ כִּי־אֵין מִרְעֶה לַצֹּאן אֲשֶׁר לַעֲבָדֶיךָ כִּי־כָבֵד הָרָעָב בְּאֶרֶץ
כְּנָעַן. וְעַתָּה יֵשְׁבוּ־נָא עֲבָדֶיךָ בְּאֶרֶץ גֹּשֶׁן.

בִּמְתֵי מְעָט. כְּמָה שֶׁנֶּאֱמַר: בְּשִׁבְעִים נֶפֶשׁ יָרְדוּ אֲבֹתֶיךָ מִצְרָיְמָה.
וְעַתָּה שָׂמְךָ יְיָ אֱלֹהֶיךָ כְּכוֹכְבֵי הַשָּׁמַיִם לָרֹב. וַיְהִי־שָׁם לְגוֹי. מְלַמֵּד
שֶׁהָיוּ יִשְׂרָאֵל מְצֻיָּנִים שָׁם. גָּדוֹל עָצוּם. כְּמָה שֶׁנֶּאֱמַר: וּבְנֵי יִשְׂרָאֵל פָּרוּ
וַיִּשְׁרְצוּ וַיִּרְבּוּ וַיַּעַצְמוּ בִּמְאֹד מְאֹד. וַתִּמָּלֵא הָאָרֶץ אֹתָם.

וָרָב. כְּמָה שֶׁנֶּאֱמַר: רְבָבָה כְּצֶמַח הַשָּׂדֶה נְתַתִּיךְ. וַתִּרְבִּי וַתִּגְדְּלִי
וַתָּבֹאִי בַּעֲדִי עֲדָיִים. שָׁדַיִם נָכֹנוּ וּשְׂעָרֵךְ צִמֵּחַ וְאַתְּ עֵרֹם וְעֶרְיָה.

וַיָּרֵעוּ אֹתָנוּ הַמִּצְרִים וַיְעַנּוּנוּ וַיִּתְּנוּ עָלֵינוּ עֲבֹדָה קָשָׁה.

וַיָּרֵעוּ אֹתָנוּ הַמִּצְרִים. כְּמָה שֶׁנֶּאֱמַר: הָבָה נִתְחַכְּמָה לוֹ. פֶּן־יִרְבֶּה
וְהָיָה כִּי־תִקְרֶאנָה מִלְחָמָה וְנוֹסַף גַּם־הוּא עַל־שֹׂנְאֵינוּ וְנִלְחַם־בָּנוּ וְעָלָה
מִן־הָאָרֶץ.

וַיְעַנּוּנוּ. כְּמָה שֶׁנֶּאֱמַר: וַיָּשִׂימוּ עָלָיו שָׂרֵי מִסִּים לְמַעַן עַנֹּתוֹ בְּסִבְלֹתָם.
וַיִּבֶן עָרֵי מִסְכְּנוֹת לְפַרְעֹה אֶת־פִּתֹם וְאֶת־רַעַמְסֵס.

וַיִּתְּנוּ עָלֵינוּ עֲבֹדָה קָשָׁה. כְּמָה שֶׁנֶּאֱמַר: וַיַּעֲבִדוּ מִצְרַיִם אֶת־בְּנֵי יִשְׂרָאֵל
בְּפָרֶךְ.

וַנִּצְעַק אֶל־יְיָ אֱלֹהֵי אֲבֹתֵינוּ. וַיִּשְׁמַע יְיָ אֶת־קֹלֵנוּ וַיַּרְא אֶת־עָנְיֵנוּ וְאֶת־עֲמָלֵנוּ וְאֶת־לַחֲצֵנוּ.

וַנִּצְעַק אֶל־יְיָ אֱלֹהֵי אֲבֹתֵינוּ. כְּמָה שֶׁנֶּאֱמַר: וַיְהִי בַיָּמִים הָרַבִּים הָהֵם וַיָּמָת מֶלֶךְ מִצְרַיִם וַיֵּאָנְחוּ בְנֵי־יִשְׂרָאֵל מִן־הָעֲבֹדָה וַיִּזְעָקוּ. וַתַּעַל שַׁוְעָתָם אֶל־הָאֱלֹהִים מִן־הָעֲבֹדָה.

וַיִּשְׁמַע יְיָ אֶת־קֹלֵנוּ. כְּמָה שֶׁנֶּאֱמַר: וַיִּשְׁמַע אֱלֹהִים אֶת־נַאֲקָתָם. וַיִּזְכֹּר אֱלֹהִים אֶת־בְּרִיתוֹ אֶת־אַבְרָהָם אֶת־יִצְחָק וְאֶת־יַעֲקֹב.

וַיַּרְא אֶת־עָנְיֵנוּ. זוֹ פְּרִישׁוּת דֶּרֶךְ אֶרֶץ. כְּמָה שֶׁנֶּאֱמַר: וַיַּרְא אֱלֹהִים אֶת־בְּנֵי יִשְׂרָאֵל וַיֵּדַע אֱלֹהִים.

וְאֶת־עֲמָלֵנוּ. אֵלוּ הַבָּנִים. כְּמָה שֶׁנֶּאֱמַר: כָּל־הַבֵּן הַיִּלּוֹד הַיְאֹרָה תַּשְׁלִיכֻהוּ וְכָל־הַבַּת תְּחַיּוּן:

וְאֶת־לַחֲצֵנוּ. זֶה הַדְּחַק. כְּמָה שֶׁנֶּאֱמַר: וְגַם־רָאִיתִי אֶת־הַלַּחַץ אֲשֶׁר מִצְרַיִם לֹחֲצִים אֹתָם.

וַיּוֹצִאֵנוּ יְיָ מִמִּצְרַיִם בְּיָד חֲזָקָה וּבִזְרֹעַ נְטוּיָה וּבְמֹרָא גָּדֹל. וּבְאֹתוֹת וּבְמֹפְתִים.

וַיּוֹצִאֵנוּ

וַיּוֹצִאֵנוּ יְיָ מִמִּצְרַיִם. לֹא־עַל־יְדֵי מַלְאָךְ. וְלֹא־עַל־יְדֵי שָׂרָף. וְלֹא־עַל־יְדֵי שָׁלִיחַ. אֶלָּא הַקָּדוֹשׁ בָּרוּךְ הוּא בִּכְבוֹדוֹ וּבְעַצְמוֹ. שֶׁנֶּאֱמַר: וְעָבַרְתִּי בְאֶרֶץ־מִצְרַיִם בַּלַּיְלָה הַזֶּה וְהִכֵּיתִי כָל־בְּכוֹר בְּאֶרֶץ מִצְרַיִם מֵאָדָם וְעַד־בְּהֵמָה. וּבְכָל־אֱלֹהֵי מִצְרַיִם אֶעֱשֶׂה שְׁפָטִים אֲנִי יְיָ.

31

עָבַרְתִּי בְאֶרֶץ־מִצְרַיִם בַּלַּיְלָה הַזֶּה. אֲנִי וְלֹא מַלְאָךְ. וְהִכֵּיתִי
כָל־בְּכוֹר בְּאֶרֶץ מִצְרַיִם. אֲנִי וְלֹא שָׂרָף. וּבְכָל־אֱלֹהֵי מִצְרַיִם אֶעֱשֶׂה
שְׁפָטִים. אֲנִי וְלֹא שָׁלִיחַ. אֲנִי יְיָ. אֲנִי הוּא וְלֹא אַחֵר.

בְּיָד חֲזָקָה. זוֹ הַדֶּבֶר. כְּמָה שֶׁנֶּאֱמַר: הִנֵּה יַד־יְיָ הוֹיָה בְּמִקְנְךָ אֲשֶׁר
בַּשָּׂדֶה בַּסּוּסִים בַּחֲמֹרִים בַּגְּמַלִּים בַּבָּקָר וּבַצֹּאן. דֶּבֶר כָּבֵד מְאֹד:

וּבִזְרֹעַ נְטוּיָה. זוֹ הַחֶרֶב. כְּמָה שֶׁנֶּאֱמַר: וְחַרְבּוֹ שְׁלוּפָה בְּיָדוֹ נְטוּיָה
עַל־יְרוּשָׁלָיִם.

וּבְמֹרָא גָּדֹל. זוֹ גִּלּוּי שְׁכִינָה. כְּמָה שֶׁנֶּאֱמַר: אוֹ הֲנִסָּה אֱלֹהִים לָבוֹא
לָקַחַת לוֹ גוֹי מִקֶּרֶב גּוֹי בְּמַסֹּת בְּאֹתֹת וּבְמוֹפְתִים וּבְמִלְחָמָה וּבְיָד חֲזָקָה
וּבִזְרוֹעַ נְטוּיָה וּבְמוֹרָאִים גְּדֹלִים. כְּכֹל אֲשֶׁר־עָשָׂה לָכֶם יְיָ אֱלֹהֵיכֶם
בְּמִצְרַיִם לְעֵינֶיךָ.

וּבְאֹתוֹת. זֶה הַמַּטֶּה. כְּמָה שֶׁנֶּאֱמַר: וְאֶת־הַמַּטֶּה הַזֶּה תִּקַּח בְּיָדֶךָ. אֲשֶׁר
תַּעֲשֶׂה־בּוֹ אֶת־הָאֹתֹת.

וּבְמֹפְתִים. זֶה הַדָּם. כְּמָה שֶׁנֶּאֱמַר: וְנָתַתִּי מוֹפְתִים בַּשָּׁמַיִם וּבָאָרֶץ.

דָּם וָאֵשׁ וְתִימְרוֹת עָשָׁן

דָּבָר אַחֵר. בְּיָד חֲזָקָה שְׁתַּיִם. וּבִזְרֹעַ נְטוּיָה שְׁתַּיִם. וּבְמֹרָא גָּדֹל
שְׁתַּיִם. וּבְאֹתוֹת שְׁתַּיִם. וּבְמֹפְתִים שְׁתַּיִם.

In The Beginning

FROM ABRAHAM TO MOSES

The leader, or a participant, continues:

In the beginning our ancestors were worshippers of idols, but as time went on they realized the folly of their ways, and the Lord drew them near to Him. In days of old, when our fathers dwelt beyond the Euphrates River, Terah, the father of Abraham, served gods of wood and stone. Abraham rebelled against the senseless practice of bowing down to the work of one's own hands, and he uprooted himself and his family and moved down to the land of Canaan. There he took unto himself Sarah as a wife, and their son Isaac was born unto them.

Isaac followed in the tradition of his father. Rebecca became his wife, and Jacob and Esau were the off-spring of their marriage.

Jacob followed in the tradition of his father and grandfather. He took unto himself Rachel and Leah as wives, and their hand-maids were Bilhah and Zilpah. The offspring of his marriages totalled twelve sons and one daughter.

A great sorrow befell Father Jacob, for he lost his beloved son Joseph, who had been sold to a caravan of Ishmaelites by his jealous brothers. Jacob, who was told by his sons that Joseph was killed by a wild beast, lived his years in grief.

A participant continues:

Once, in Egypt, Joseph was resold as a slave to Potifar, vizier of Pharaoh and keeper of the palace. For many years Joseph languished in prison until, through an act of Providence, he was enabled to display his wisdom to the butler of the king who, like Joseph, was a fellow prisoner.

One day, after the butler had been freed and resumed his post in the court of the king, Pharaoh was troubled by dreams that none of his wise men could interpret for him. It was then that the butler remembered Joseph, and he told the king about the imprisoned young Hebrew lad who had been successful in interpreting dreams.

Another participant continues:

Joseph was brought before the king, and he satisfied the king's disquietude by interpreting for him, and explaining, the significance of the dreams that troubled him. From that moment on, Joseph rose in power and prestige. Pharaoh said to him: "You shall rule over my house, and to you all my people will pay homage; only I and my throne will be more exalted than you."

Having reached this position, Joseph was now determined to bring his father from Canaan down to the land of Egypt. A dreadful famine had engulfed the land of Canaan, and only in the land of Egypt was food plentiful. After many trying and agonizing episodes, Joseph finally revealed himself to his brothers. Soon thereafter Jacob and his family moved to Egypt.

A special city was set aside for the family of Jacob, and it was named Goshen. In the city of Goshen, in the land of Egypt, Jacob and his offspring dwelled in peace and plenty.

Another participant continues:

Seventy persons were they who came down to Egypt with Father Jacob, and soon they increased and multiplied. It was as if the land was filled with the descendants of Jacob.

Before long, Father Jacob died and, then, Joseph died, too. A new king ascended the throne of Egypt. The new Pharaoh viewed with apprehension the ever increasing number of Hebrews who were becoming mighty and influential. He chose to forget Joseph and all that he had done to save Egypt in the years of severe famine.

Pharaoh said to his people: "Behold, the children of Israel are too many and too mighty for us! Let us reconsider their position, lest they multiply even more, and grow ever more powerful! Should a war come, it may very well be that they will join our enemies and flee from the country."

And so, it was henceforth decreed that all Hebrews be carefully watched and their power curbed. All their newborn sons were to be thrown into the river so that the nation might not reproduce itself, and all adults were to become slaves of the Crown.

And so it was that the children of Israel were forced into slavery, and for long hours each day they toiled in the fields, gathering straw and then making the bricks to build the great monuments and pyramids that were to attest to the eternity of the Pharaohs.

Another participant continues:

But one Hebrew baby was hidden among the reeds of the river. When the king's daughter went down to the river-edge for her daily bath, she heard the cry of the young child and sent her handmaids to fetch it. And she loved the child and took him to the castle and called him Moses, meaning, "I drew him forth from the water." Under the protective custody of the oppressor himself, Moses, the son of a Hebrew, grew into manhood. And as he grew, so did his sympathy for the lot of his suffering people. In time, he renounced his royal privileges, and became the protagonist of his fellow Hebrews, crushed by the yoke of slavery.

To escape the wrath of the king, he fled to the desert of Sinai, and there within the secrecy of his own soul, he found the purpose and destiny of his life. In the burning bush that would not be consumed, despite the fiery flames that engulfed it, he saw the answer to his bewilderment. This was surely a message from the Almighty, saying to him: Whatever is worthwhile cannot be destroyed! Whatever is good and right must be defended! Was not this a call to return to his brethren? Was not this a message from Above declaring that he must dedicate his life to the liberation of his people?

Back to the fiery cauldron of Egypt did he go, and there with his brother Aaron did he confront the king. "Let my people go," he cried, "that they may serve their God!"

At some Seder celebrations the participants may want to join in singing the following well-known spiritual which epitomizes the ancient struggle of the Israelites in Egypt.

LET MY PEOPLE GO

When Israel was in Egypt land,
Let my people go.

Oppressed so hard they could not stand,
Let my people go.

REFRAIN

Go down, Moses, way down in Egypt land,
Tell ol' Pharaoh, let my people go.

Thus saith the Lord, bold Moses said,
Let my people go.

If not I'll smite your people dead,
Let my people go.   (Refrain)

As Israel stood by the water side,
Let my people go.

By God's command it did divide,
Let my people go.   (Refrain)

36

A participant continues:

Again and again Moses demanded, "Let my people go! Let my people go, that they may hold a festival in God's honor in the desert!"

But Pharaoh refused, again and again, saying, "Who is the Lord that I should listen to Him? I know not your God. I will not let Israel go!"

Moses appealed to the Lord and said: "O Lord, why hast Thou ill-treated this people? Why didst Thou send me here? Ever since I came to Pharaoh to speak in Thy Name, he has added to the burdens of this people and Thou hast done nothing to rescue them!"

And God answered: "I have heard the groaning of the children of Israel and I have paid heed to their cries. Go to them and tell them: 'I am the Lord! I will free them from the burden of the Egyptians, and I will remove from them the yoke of their bondage.' "

But Pharaoh was not moved, and God brought the Ten Plagues upon Egypt.

The Ten Plagues

It is customary for each participant to pour off wine from his cup, into the saucer, as each of the Ten Plagues is mentioned. Usually, the spoon is dipped into the wine, and a drop or two is placed in the saucer.

This practice has been explained as an expression of our unhappiness over the misfortune suffered by the Egyptians. In very poetic language the Talmud puts it this way: "When the Egyptians were drowning, the Angels wished to sing. But God said, 'My handiwork is drowning and you wish to sing!'" The thought of rejoicing over the suffering of others is alien to Judaism, even where the punishment may be justified.

All recite in unison:

אֵלּוּ. עֶשֶׂר מַכּוֹת שֶׁהֵבִיא
הַקָּדוֹשׁ בָּרוּךְ הוּא עַל
מִצְרַיִם וְאֵלּוּ הֵן.

Aylu eser makōs she-hayvee Hakodōsh Boruch Hu al ha-Mitzrim b'Mitzro-yim, v'aylu hayn:

These are the ten plagues that God brought to afflict the Egyptians:

1. Dom   דָּם

BLOOD

And the Lord said to Moses, "Say unto Aaron: 'Take thy rod, and stretch out thy hand over the waters of Egypt, over their rivers, over their streams, over their pools, and over their ponds, that they may become blood. And there shall be blood throughout all the land of Egypt . . .'" And Moses and Aaron did as the Lord had commanded . . . And all the waters that were in the river were turned to blood. (Exodus 7:19-20)

2. Tz'farday-a

צְפַרְדֵּעַ

FROGS

And the Lord said to Moses, "Say unto Aaron: 'Stretch forth thy hand with thy rod over the rivers, over the canals, and over the pools, and cause frogs to come up upon the land of Egypt.' " And Aaron stretched out his hand over the waters of Egypt, and the frogs came up and covered the land of Egypt. (Exodus 8:1-2)

3. Keenim

כִּנִּים

LICE

And the Lord said to Moses, "Say unto Aaron: 'Stretch out thy rod, and smite the dust of the earth, that it may become lice throughout all the land of Egypt.' " And he did so. And Aaron stretched out his hand with his rod, and smote the dust of the earth, and there were lice upon man, and upon beast. All the dust of the earth turned into lice throughout all the land of Egypt. (Exodus 8:12-13)

4. Orov

עָרוֹב

WILD BEASTS

And there came grievous hordes of wild beasts into the house of Pharaoh, and into his servants' houses. And the whole land of Egypt was ruined because of the hordes of beasts. (Exodus 8:20)

5. Dever

דֶּבֶר

CATTLE PLAGUE

The Lord said to Moses, "Go tell Pharaoh: 'Let My people go, that they may serve Me! For, if thou refuse to let them go, behold the hand of the Lord is upon thy cattle which are in the field; upon the asses, upon the camels, upon the herds and upon the flocks. There shall be a very grievous plague among your cattle.' " (Exodus 9:1-3)

6. Sh'chin

שְׁחִין

BOILS

And the Lord said to Moses and Aaron, "Take handfuls of soot from the furnace, and let Moses throw it heavenward in the sight of Pharaoh. And it shall become fine dust covering the land of Egypt. And it shall cause boils to break forth upon man and beast." (Exodus 9:8-9)

7. Borod

בָּרָד

HAIL

And Moses stretched forth his rod toward heaven, and the Lord sent thunder and hail. And flashing fire descended into the earth, and hail rained upon the land of Egypt. So there was hail, and a flashing fire in the midst of the hail, such as had not been seen in the land of Egypt since it had become a nation. And the hail smote all that was in the field, both man and beast. Every herb of the field was smitten, and every tree was broken. (Exodus 9:23-25)

8. Arbeh

אַרְבֶּה

LOCUSTS

And Moses stretched forth his rod over the land of Egypt, and the Lord brought an east wind upon the land, all that day and all that night; and when it was morning, the east wind brought the locusts . . . They covered the face of the whole earth . . . and ate every herb of the land, and all the fruit of the trees which the hail had left. And there remained not one green thing—neither tree nor herb—in the whole land of Egypt. (Exodus 10:12-15)

9. Choshech

חשֶׁךְ

DARKNESS

And Moses stretched forth his rod toward heaven, and there was deep darkness in all the land of Egypt for three days. They could not see one another, nor could they move from their places for three days, but all the Children of Israel had light in their dwellings. (Exodus 11:22-23)

10. Makas B'choros

מַכַּת בְּכוֹרוֹת

SLAYING OF FIRST-BORN

And it came to pass at midnight, that the Lord smote all the first-born in the land of Egypt, from the first-born of Pharaoh that sat on the throne to the first born of the captive that was in the dungeon, and all the first-born of the cattle . . . And there was a great cry in Egypt, for there was not a house without its dead. (Exodus 12:29)

And Pharaoh rose up and called Moses and Aaron and said: "Rise up, get ye forth, both ye and the Children of Israel, and go serve the Lord as ye have demanded." (Exodus 12:30-31)

רַבִּי יְהוּדָה הָיָה נוֹתֵן בָּהֶם סִמָּנִים:

דְּצַ"ךְ, עֲדַ"שׁ, בְּאַחַ"ב.

רַבִּי יוֹסֵי הַגְּלִילִי אוֹמֵר. מִנַּיִן אַתָּה אוֹמֵר שֶׁלָּקוּ הַמִּצְרִים בְּמִצְרַיִם עֶשֶׂר מַכּוֹת. וְעַל־הַיָּם לָקוּ חֲמִשִּׁים מַכּוֹת. בְּמִצְרַיִם מַה הוּא אוֹמֵר. וַיֹּאמְרוּ הַחַרְטֻמִּים אֶל־פַּרְעֹה אֶצְבַּע אֱלֹהִים הִיא: וְעַל הַיָּם מַה־הוּא אוֹמֵר. וַיַּרְא יִשְׂרָאֵל אֶת־הַיָּד הַגְּדֹלָה אֲשֶׁר עָשָׂה יְיָ בְּמִצְרַיִם וַיִּירְאוּ הָעָם אֶת־יְיָ וַיַּאֲמִינוּ בַּייָ וּבְמֹשֶׁה עַבְדּוֹ. כַּמָּה לָקוּ בְּאֶצְבַּע. עֶשֶׂר מַכּוֹת. אֱמוֹר מֵעַתָּה בְּמִצְרַיִם לָקוּ עֶשֶׂר מַכּוֹת וְעַל־הַיָּם לָקוּ חֲמִשִּׁים מַכּוֹת.

The question as to whether miracles are possible has long been a subject of debate. A miracle, by definition, is a deviation from the established laws of nature. The Midrash, which contains the thinking of the early rabbis (1st to 5th centuries) expresses the view, which is generally accepted in Judaism, that the miracles described in the Bible were not "miraculous" events, but were pre-ordained. Hence, rather than constituting a break with natural law, they were actually a fulfillment of natural law.

The Midrash puts it this way: Rabbi Johanan said, "God made an agreement with the sea (when He created it during the period of creation) that it should split in half when it would be approached by the Israelites (fleeing from Egypt)."

Rabbi Jeremiah said: "God not only made an agreement with the sea, but He made an agreement with all the other things that were created during the six days of creation."

And Rabbi Jeremiah goes on to say:

"God made an agreement with the sun and the moon that they should stand still in the time of Joshua."

"God made an agreement with the ravens that they should feed Elijah."

"God made an agreement with the fire that it should not harm Hananiah, Mishael and Azariah, the three friends of Daniel, when they would be thrown into the fiery furnace at the command of Nebuchadnezzar of Babylonia.

"God made an agreement with the fish that it should spit out Jonah alive, after it had swallowed him."

What is the Midrash trying to tell us when it enumerates all these events which we speak of as miracles? The Midrash is saying, quite obviously, that none of these were breaks in the workings of nature. Nature does not violate its own laws.

George Santayana summed it up as follows: "Miracles are propitious accidents, the natural causes of which are too complicated to be clearly understood."

רַבִּי אֱלִיעֶזֶר אוֹמֵר. מִנַּיִן שֶׁכָּל מַכָּה וּמַכָּה שֶׁהֵבִיא הַקָּדוֹשׁ בָּרוּךְ
הוּא עַל הַמִּצְרִים בְּמִצְרַיִם הָיְתָה שֶׁל אַרְבַּע מַכּוֹת. שֶׁנֶּאֱמַר: יְשַׁלַּח
בָּם חֲרוֹן אַפּוֹ עֶבְרָה וָזַעַם וְצָרָה מִשְׁלַחַת מַלְאֲכֵי רָעִים: עֶבְרָה אַחַת.
וָזַעַם שְׁתַּיִם. וְצָרָה שָׁלֹשׁ. מִשְׁלַחַת מַלְאֲכֵי רָעִים אַרְבַּע. אֱמוֹר מֵעַתָּה.
בְּמִצְרַיִם לָקוּ אַרְבָּעִים מַכּוֹת וְעַל הַיָּם לָקוּ מָאתַיִם מַכּוֹת.

רַבִּי עֲקִיבָא אוֹמֵר. מִנַּיִן שֶׁכָּל מַכָּה וּמַכָּה שֶׁהֵבִיא הַקָּדוֹשׁ בָּרוּךְ הוּא
עַל הַמִּצְרִים בְּמִצְרַיִם הָיְתָה שֶׁל חָמֵשׁ מַכּוֹת. שֶׁנֶּאֱמַר: יְשַׁלַּח־בָּם חֲרוֹן
אַפּוֹ עֶבְרָה וָזַעַם וְצָרָה מִשְׁלַחַת מַלְאֲכֵי רָעִים. חֲרוֹן אַפּוֹ אַחַת. עֶבְרָה
שְׁתַּיִם. וָזַעַם שָׁלֹשׁ. וְצָרָה אַרְבַּע. מִשְׁלַחַת מַלְאֲכֵי רָעִים חָמֵשׁ. אֱמוֹר
מֵעַתָּה. בְּמִצְרַיִם לָקוּ חֲמִשִּׁים מַכּוֹת וְעַל הַיָּם לָקוּ חֲמִשִּׁים וּמָאתַיִם
מַכּוֹת.

דַּיֵּנוּ.

How Grateful And Content (Da-yaynu)

Leader:

How grateful and content are we, for all Thy beneficence, O
Lord!

For sparing our ancestors of old from the disastrous plagues that
befell the Egyptians, we are grateful and content.

For strengthening our martyrs of latter days, to face with courage the demonic forces that took their lives, we are grateful and
filled with pride.

דַּיֵּנוּ דַּיֵּנוּ דַּיֵּנוּ.

DA-YAYNU

All join in singing these selected portions in
either the Hebrew or English:

(Refrain)

Da-da-yaynu	We would have been grateful
Da-da-yaynu	We would have been grateful
Da-da-yaynu	We would have been grateful
Da-yaynu, da-yaynu.	Grateful and content.

Eelu hō-tzee-onu mee-Mitzra-yim

    Da-yaynu.

Had He done no more,
  Than save us from Egypt.
    We would have been content.

Eelu nosan lonu es ha-Shabos

    Da-yaynu.

Had He done nothing else,
  But give us the Sabbath rest.
    We would have been content.

Eelu nosan lonu es HaTōrah

    Da-yaynu.

Had He blessed us only,
  With the Torah holy.
    We would have been content.

44

כַּמָּה מַעֲלוֹת טוֹבוֹת לַמָּקוֹם עָלֵינוּ

אִלּוּ הוֹצִיאָנוּ מִמִּצְרַיִם

וְלֹא עָשָׂה בָהֶם שְׁפָטִים   דַּיֵּנוּ.

אִלּוּ עָשָׂה בָהֶם שְׁפָטִים

וְלֹא עָשָׂה בֵאלֹהֵיהֶם   דַּיֵּנוּ.

אִלּוּ עָשָׂה בֵאלֹהֵיהֶם

וְלֹא הָרַג בְּכוֹרֵיהֶם   דַּיֵּנוּ.

אִלּוּ הָרַג בְּכוֹרֵיהֶם

וְלֹא נָתַן לָנוּ אֶת־מָמוֹנָם   דַּיֵּנוּ.

אִלּוּ נָתַן לָנוּ אֶת־מָמוֹנָם

וְלֹא קָרַע לָנוּ אֶת־הַיָּם   דַּיֵּנוּ.

אִלּוּ קָרַע לָנוּ אֶת־הַיָּם

וְלֹא הֶעֱבִירָנוּ בְתוֹכוֹ בֶּחָרָבָה   דַּיֵּנוּ.

אִלּוּ הֶעֱבִירָנוּ בְתוֹכוֹ בֶּחָרָבָה

וְלֹא שִׁקַּע צָרֵינוּ בְּתוֹכוֹ   דַּיֵּנוּ.

אִלּוּ שִׁקַּע צָרֵינוּ בְּתוֹכוֹ

וְלֹא סִפֵּק צָרְכֵּנוּ בַּמִּדְבָּר אַרְבָּעִים שָׁנָה   דַּיֵּנוּ.

אִלּוּ סִפֵּק צָרְכֵּנוּ בַּמִּדְבָּר אַרְבָּעִים שָׁנָה

וְלֹא הֶאֱכִילָנוּ אֶת־הַמָּן   דַּיֵּנוּ.

אִלּוּ הֶאֱכִילָנוּ אֶת־הַמָּן

וְלֹא נָתַן לָנוּ אֶת־הַשַּׁבָּת   דַּיֵּנוּ.

אִלּוּ נָתַן לָנוּ אֶת הַשַּׁבָּת

וְלֹא קֵרְבָנוּ לִפְנֵי הַר סִינַי — דַּיֵּנוּ.

אִלּוּ קֵרְבָנוּ לִפְנֵי הַר סִינַי

וְלֹא נָתַן לָנוּ אֶת הַתּוֹרָה — דַּיֵּנוּ.

אִלּוּ נָתַן לָנוּ אֶת הַתּוֹרָה

וְלֹא הִכְנִיסָנוּ לְאֶרֶץ יִשְׂרָאֵל — דַּיֵּנוּ.

אִלּוּ הִכְנִיסָנוּ לְאֶרֶץ יִשְׂרָאֵל

וְלֹא בָנָה לָנוּ אֶת בֵּית הַבְּחִירָה — דַּיֵּנוּ.

RESPONSIVE READING

Participants: For all Thy acts of kindness,
We are most grateful and content.

Leader: If Thy only act of kindness
Was to deliver us from the bondage of Egypt,

Participants: We would have been grateful and content.

Leader: If Thy only act of deliverance
Was the bringing of the plagues,

Participants: We would have been grateful and content.

Leader: If Thy only act of mercy
Was to divide the Red Sea waters,

Participants: We would have been grateful and content.

Leader: If Thy only act of mercy
Was to provide the Manna in the desert,

Participants: We would have been grateful and content.

Leader: If Thy only act of graciousness
Was the gift of a Sabbath day,

Participants:	We would have been grateful and content.
Leader:	If Thy only act of love Was to favor us with Thy Torah,
Participants:	We would have been grateful and content.
Leader:	If Thy only act of loving-kindness Was to bring us into the Land of Israel,
Participants:	We would have been grateful and content.

All recite in unison:

עַל אַחַת כַּמָּה וְכַמָּה, טוֹבָה כְפוּלָה
וּמְכֻפֶּלֶת, לַמָּקוֹם עָלֵינוּ. שֶׁהוֹצִיאָנוּ
מִמִּצְרַיִם. וְעָשָׂה בָהֶם שְׁפָטִים. וְעָשָׂה
בֵאלֹהֵיהֶם. וְהָרַג אֶת בְּכוֹרֵיהֶם. וְנָתַן לָנוּ
אֶת מָמוֹנָם. וְקָרַע לָנוּ אֶת הַיָּם. וְהֶעֱבִירָנוּ
בְתוֹכוֹ בֶּחָרָבָה. וְשִׁקַּע צָרֵינוּ בְּתוֹכוֹ. וְסִפֵּק
צָרְכֵּנוּ בַּמִּדְבָּר אַרְבָּעִים שָׁנָה. וְהֶאֱכִילָנוּ
אֶת הַמָּן. וְנָתַן לָנוּ אֶת הַשַּׁבָּת. וְקֵרְבָנוּ לִפְנֵי
הַר סִינַי. וְנָתַן לָנוּ אֶת הַתּוֹרָה. וְהִכְנִיסָנוּ
לְאֶרֶץ יִשְׂרָאֵל . וּבָנָה לָנוּ אֶת בֵּית הַבְּחִירָה
לְכַפֵּר עַל כָּל עֲוֹנוֹתֵינוּ.

"We have not journeyed all this way across the centuries, across the mountains, across the prairies, because we are made of sugar candy."

WINSTON S. CHURCHILL

How grateful are we, and how doubly blessed, for all these acts of kindness and mercy and grace which The Lord our God has bestowed upon us through His acts of beneficence to our ancestors.

He redeemed them from Egypt and punished their enemies.

He made a mockery of their gods, and took a toll of their first-born.

He repaid us from their wealth for the years of slavery in Egypt.

He split the waters of the Red Sea, and permitted us to pass through in safety.

He sent our oppressors to their doom, and provided us with Manna in the desert.

He bequeathed unto us a Sabbath day, and permitted us to approach Mount Sinai.

He blessed us with His Torah, and guided us to the Land of Israel where we built the holy Temple.

רַבָּן גַּמְלִיאֵל הָיָה אוֹמֵר. כָּל־שֶׁלֹּא אָמַר
שְׁלֹשָׁה דְבָרִים אֵלּוּ בְּפֶסַח. לֹא יָצָא יְדֵי
חוֹבָתוֹ. וְאֵלּוּ הֵן:

פֶּסַח

מַצָּה

מָרוֹר

Leader:

Studying the events of the Passover story, Rabbi Gamliel observed:

There are three distinctive elements which must be acknowledged and preserved, through rite and ceremony, if a Jew is to fulfill his duty on this Seder eve. He must recognize the significance of the *matzo,* the paschal lamb and the bitter herbs. These three elements are all interwoven in the fabric of the Exodus drama, and each symbolizes the effort and idealism with which the achievement of true freedom and liberation must be invested.

49

PESACH — The Paschal Lamb

MATZO — The Unleavened Bread

MOROR — The Bitter Herbs

What do these elements symbolize, and what is their significance?

Leader raises the bone on the Seder dish which is symbolic of
the lamb that was originally eaten on Passover, and all the
celebrants recite in unison:

פֶּ סַ ח שֶׁהָיוּ אֲבוֹתֵינוּ אוֹכְלִים, בִּזְמַן שֶׁבֵּית
הַמִּקְדָּשׁ קַיָּם, עַל שׁוּם מָה. עַל שׁוּם, שֶׁפָּסַח
הַקָּדוֹשׁ בָּרוּךְ הוּא, עַל בָּתֵּי אֲבוֹתֵינוּ
בְּמִצְרַיִם. שֶׁנֶּאֱמַר: וַאֲמַרְתֶּם זֶבַח פֶּסַח הוּא
לַיָי, אֲשֶׁר פָּסַח, עַל בָּתֵּי בְנֵי יִשְׂרָאֵל
בְּמִצְרַיִם, בְּנָגְפּוֹ אֶת מִצְרַיִם, וְאֶת בָּתֵּינוּ
הִצִּיל. וַיִּקֹּד הָעָם וַיִּשְׁתַּחֲווּ.

PESACH — The paschal lamb that was once eaten on Passover
eve, in the days when the Temple stood in Jerusalem, and when
sacrifices were offered on the altar—of what does it remind us,
and what does it teach us?

It reminds us of the tenth plague in Egypt, when all the first-
born of the Egyptians were struck down. It reminds us of the
salvation of the Israelites whose homes were spared. For *pesach*
means not only paschal lamb—it has another meaning as well. It
means, "He skipped over." The Lord skipped over the homes of
the Israelites whose doorposts had been dabbed with the blood
of the sacrificial lamb.

The willingness to sacrifice is the prelude to freedom.

The first step in the struggle to lift the yoke of bondage must be marked with the blood of idealism—of idealistic men and women who are willing to make the sacrifice that the realization of freedom requires. Liberty is not achieved by complacency; it is not won without suffering the scars of battle. It is accomplished by selflessness and sacrifice; it is won by courageous action. Thus do we bow before the Lord our Maker; thus do we perform His will.

The leader replaces the bone and holds up the *Matzo*, and all recite in unison:

מַ **צָּה** זוֹ שֶׁאָנוּ אוֹכְלִים עַל שׁוּם מָה. עַל שׁוּם, שֶׁלֹּא הִסְפִּיק בְּצֵקָם שֶׁל אֲבוֹתֵינוּ לְהַחֲמִיץ, עַד שֶׁנִּגְלָה עֲלֵיהֶם, מֶלֶךְ מַלְכֵי הַמְּלָכִים הַקָּדוֹשׁ בָּרוּךְ הוּא, וּגְאָלָם. שֶׁנֶּאֱמַר: וַיֹּאפוּ אֶת הַבָּצֵק, אֲשֶׁר הוֹצִיאוּ מִמִּצְרַיִם, עֻגֹת מַצּוֹת כִּי לֹא חָמֵץ. כִּי גֹרְשׁוּ מִמִּצְרַיִם, וְלֹא יָכְלוּ לְהִתְמַהְמֵהַּ, וְגַם צֵדָה לֹא עָשׂוּ לָהֶם.

MATZO — This *matzo* that we eat on Passover—what is its meaning and what is its significance?

The *matzo* is a reminder of the haste with which the Israelites left Egypt. The dough that they were sunbaking on the hot rocks of the Egyptian fields was removed before it could leaven, and it remained flat.

What does this teach us, and what is its significance, as we celebrate this holiday of freedom? It teaches us that liberty is achieved not by sacrifice alone, for sacrifice must be accompanied by alertness, by readiness. To aspire towards freedom, we must be prepared to seize opportunities as they arise. To overlook the

51

opportunity, to miss the chance, because we are not prepared to move quickly and decisively when the blow for freedom can be struck, is to betray the will of God and the hope of mankind.

The Leader replaces the *Matzo* and holds up the bitter herbs, and all recite in unison:

מָרוֹר זֶה שֶׁאָנוּ אוֹכְלִים עַל שׁוּם מָה.

עַל שׁוּם, שֶׁמֵּרְרוּ הַמִּצְרִים אֶת חַיֵּי אֲבוֹתֵינוּ

בְּמִצְרָיִם. שֶׁנֶּאֱמַר: וַיְמָרְרוּ אֶת חַיֵּיהֶם

בַּעֲבֹדָה קָשָׁה, בְּחֹמֶר וּבִלְבֵנִים, וּבְכָל

עֲבֹדָה בַּשָּׂדֶה. אֵת כָּל עֲבֹדָתָם, אֲשֶׁר עָבְדוּ

בָהֶם בְּפָרֶךְ.

MOROR — These bitter herbs that we eat on Passover—what is their origin and what is their meaning?

The bitter herbs symbolize the bitter lot of the Israelites who were enslaved in Egypt. They remind us of the forced labor the children of Israel were compelled to perform in the sun-drenched fields of Egypt under the lash of the Egyptian taskmaster. Their lot was bitter, but they endured the misery and did not succumb, for the hope of redemption was kept alive by their great leader Moses, who persisted in his battle to overthrow the tyrant.

Sacrifice and readiness must be accompanied by a dedicated leadership that keeps the spark of hope alive, if tyranny is to be overthrown and freedom is to be won. The bitterness of one's lot at a given moment must never be allowed to develop into defeatism.

"These are times that try men's souls . . . what we obtain too cheap, we esteem too lightly; 'tis dearness only that gives everything its value. Heaven knows how to put a proper price upon its goods; and it would be strange indeed, if so celestial an article as *Freedom* should not be highly rated."

THOMAS PAINE

52

Pesach, Matzo and *Moror* are the symbolic expressions that represent freedom in all ages. Translated into modern terms, they are sacrifice, preparedness and hope. These are the elements that are necessary in the battle of freedom. And any Jew who does not recognize the importance of these elements is not a true Jew. Any human being who does not understand their significance is not truly human.

A participant continues:

It therefore becomes the sacred obligation of every parent to be a teacher—to teach his child the meaning of freedom, so that it will be learned anew. As it is written: "On that day shalt thou teach thy son, saying, 'It is because of this (leader points to the symbols on the table) that God delivered *me* from Egypt.' " Because of *Pesach, Matzo* and *Moror* did redemption come to us.

Not only our forefathers alone did God redeem from Egypt! We, too, were redeemed; we, too, were with them in spirit. Each of us, living today, is a beneficiary of the struggle and salvation of ages gone by.

בְּכָל דּוֹר וָדוֹר חַיָּב אָדָם לִרְאוֹת אֶת־עַצְמוֹ, כְּאִלוּ הוּא יָצָא מִמִּצְרַיִם. שֶׁנֶּאֱמַר: וְהִגַּדְתָּ לְבִנְךָ, בַּיּוֹם הַהוּא לֵאמֹר. בַּעֲבוּר זֶה, עָשָׂה יְיָ לִי, בְּצֵאתִי מִמִּצְרָיִם. לֹא אֶת־אֲבוֹתֵינוּ בִּלְבַד גָּאַל הַקָּדוֹשׁ בָּרוּךְ הוּא, אֶלָּא אַף אוֹתָנוּ גָּאַל עִמָּהֶם. שֶׁנֶּאֱמַר: וְאוֹתָנוּ הוֹצִיא מִשָּׁם. לְמַעַן הָבִיא אֹתָנוּ, לָתֶת לָנוּ אֶת־הָאָרֶץ, אֲשֶׁר נִשְׁבַּע לַאֲבוֹתֵינוּ.

B'chol dōr vodōr cha-yov odom lirōs es atzmō k'eelu hu yotzo mee-Mitzro-yim.

Leader:

In every generation it is the duty of each of us to imagine that it is we—we ourselves—who were saved from the bondage of Egypt. For it is written: "And thou shalt tell thy son on that day, 'It is because of that which the Lord did for *me* when I came forth out of Egypt.'" Not only our forefathers, did the Holy One, Blessed be He, redeem; He liberated us along with them. Thus, the answer to all defiant and doubting sons is this: Passover becomes real only when it is personal; freedom becomes real only when we identify *ourselves* with it and strive to spread its fruits to all people, everywhere.

"When we are planning for posterity, we ought to remember that virtue is not hereditary."

THOMAS PAINE

54

Participants raise their cups of wine and recite in unison:

פִיכָךְ אֲנַחְנוּ חַיָּבִים לְהוֹדוֹת, לְהַלֵּל, לְשַׁבֵּחַ, לְפָאֵר, לְרוֹמֵם, לְהַדֵּר, לְבָרֵךְ, לְעַלֵּה וּלְקַלֵּס לְמִי שֶׁעָשָׂה לַאֲבוֹתֵינוּ וְלָנוּ אֶת כָּל הַנִּסִּים הָאֵלֶּה. הוֹצִיאָנוּ מֵעַבְדוּת לְחֵרוּת, מִיָּגוֹן לְשִׂמְחָה, מֵאֵבֶל לְיוֹם טוֹב, וּמֵאֲפֵלָה לְאוֹר גָּדוֹל, וּמִשִּׁעְבּוּד לִגְאֻלָּה. וְנֹאמַר לְפָנָיו שִׁירָה חֲדָשָׁה. הַלְלוּיָה.

And thus do we raise our voices in words of thanks and praise to the Lord our God who saw fit to bring salvation and freedom to our oppressed ancestors. Miraculously did He take them out of the savage bondage of Egypt, and bring them into a new life with its promise of freedom and equality. He converted their sadness into joy; their mourning into gladness; and their dark future into a great light of hope. For all His goodness, for His great gift of redemption, we raise our voices in songs of praise. Halleluyah!

Cups are replaced on the table.

Hallel (Psalms of Praise)

Six psalms from the Book of Psalms (113-118) are recited during the Seder service. Two are recited at this time, before the
meal, and four after the meal. According to the Talmud, these
psalms were chanted by the Levites, in Temple days, while the
paschal lamb was being offered on the altar, by the priests.

PSALM 113

Psalm 113 expresses hope for the ultimate, personal salvation
of all who are distressed and downtrodden. The psalm may be
recited responsively.

הַלְלוּיָה הַלְלוּ עַבְדֵי יְיָ. הַלְלוּ אֶת־שֵׁם יְיָ.

יְהִי שֵׁם יְיָ מְבֹרָךְ מֵעַתָּה וְעַד עוֹלָם.

מִמִּזְרַח־שֶׁמֶשׁ עַד־מְבוֹאוֹ מְהֻלָּל שֵׁם יְיָ.

רָם עַל־כָּל־גּוֹיִם יְיָ עַל־הַשָּׁמַיִם כְּבוֹדוֹ.

מִי כַּיְיָ אֱלֹהֵינוּ הַמַּגְבִּיהִי לָשָׁבֶת.

הַמַּשְׁפִּילִי לִרְאוֹת בַּשָּׁמַיִם וּבָאָרֶץ.

מְקִימִי מֵעָפָר דָּל מֵאַשְׁפֹּת יָרִים אֶבְיוֹן.

לְהוֹשִׁיבִי עִם־נְדִיבִים עִם נְדִיבֵי עַמּוֹ.

מוֹשִׁיבִי עֲקֶרֶת הַבַּיִת אֵם הַבָּנִים שְׂמֵחָה הַלְלוּיָה.

Halleluyah! Praise the name of the Lord,
O ye servants of the Lord.

From the rising of the sun
Until its setting,
Give praise to the name of the Lord.

Supreme above all nations is the Lord,
His majesty extends above the very heavens.

Who can compare to the Lord,
Who is like unto our God
Enthroned on high?

From the glory of His heights
He looks down upon heaven and earth.

He raises the poor
Out of the dust;
The needy out of the mire.

He seats them among princes,
Among princes of His people.

Even to those who are barren
Does He bring His blessing,
As a joyful mother of children.
Halleluyah!

PSALM 114

Psalm 114 offers, in graphic and picturesque language, a description of
how all nature joyously joined in helping the fleeing Israelites win their
freedom, as they escaped from the hordes of pursuing Egyptians. The psalm
may be recited responsively.

בְּצֵאת יִשְׂרָאֵל מִמִּצְרָיִם בֵּית יַעֲקֹב מֵעַם לֹעֵז.

הָיְתָה יְהוּדָה לְקָדְשׁוֹ יִשְׂרָאֵל מַמְשְׁלוֹתָיו.

הַיָּם רָאָה וַיָּנֹס הַיַּרְדֵּן יִסֹּב לְאָחוֹר.

הֶהָרִים רָקְדוּ כְאֵילִים גְּבָעוֹת כִּבְנֵי־צֹאן.

מַה לְּךָ הַיָּם כִּי תָנוּס הַיַּרְדֵּן תִּסֹּב לְאָחוֹר.

הֶהָרִים תִּרְקְדוּ כְאֵילִים גְּבָעוֹת כִּבְנֵי־צֹאן.

מִלִּפְנֵי אָדוֹן חוּלִי אָרֶץ מִלִּפְנֵי אֱלוֹהַּ יַעֲקֹב.

הַהֹפְכִי הַצּוּר אֲגַם־מָיִם חַלָּמִישׁ לְמַעְיְנוֹ מָיִם.

57

When Israel was delivered from Egypt,
The House of Jacob from a foreign oppressor;

The territory of Judah was to become his sanctuary,
The land of Israel his sacred domicile.

The sea saw the redemption and it fled,
The Jordan turned back in its course.

The mountains shook like frightened rams,
The hills danced like fearful lambs.

Why is it, O sea, that you flee?
Why, O Jordan, do you turn backward?

Why, O mountains, do you prance like rams?
O, you hills, like fearful lambs?

You do have cause to tremble, O earth,
To tremble before the powerful God of Jacob!

For it was He who turned rock into water,
Lifeless stone into a flowing fountain.

All participants raise their wine goblets and read in unison:

בָּרוּך אַתָּה יְיָ אֱלֹהֵינוּ מֶלֶך הָעוֹלָם אֲשֶׁר גְּאָלָנוּ וְגָאַל אֶת־אֲבוֹתֵינוּ

מִמִּצְרַיִם וְהִגִּיעָנוּ הַלַּיְלָה הַזֶּה לֶאֱכָל בּוֹ מַצָּה וּמָרוֹר. כֵּן יְיָ אֱלֹהֵינוּ

וֵאלֹהֵי אֲבוֹתֵינוּ הַגִּיעֵנוּ לְמוֹעֲדִים וְלִרְגָלִים אֲחֵרִים הַבָּאִים לִקְרָאתֵנוּ

לְשָׁלוֹם שְׂמֵחִים בְּבִנְיַן עִירֶךָ וְשָׂשִׂים בַּעֲבוֹדָתֶךָ. וְנֹאכַל שָׁם מִן

הַזְּבָחִים וּמִן הַפְּסָחִים אֲשֶׁר יַגִּיעַ דָּמָם עַל קִיר מִזְבַּחֲךָ לְרָצוֹן.

וְנוֹדֶה לְךָ שִׁיר חָדָשׁ עַל־גְּאֻלָּתֵנוּ וְעַל פְּדוּת נַפְשֵׁנוּ . בָּרוּך אַתָּה יְיָ

גָּאַל יִשְׂרָאֵל.

Praised be Thou, O Lord our God, King of the universe, Who redeemed us and our fathers from Egypt, and brought us to this night on which we eat unleavened bread and bitter herbs. Thus, O Lord our God, and God of our fathers, do Thou enable us to enjoy other holidays and festivals, in peace, rejoicing in the building of Thy city and delighting in Thy service. Ever will we thank Thee through new songs of redemption and deliverance. Praised be Thou, O Lord, Who has redeemed Israel.

בָּרוּךְ אַתָּה יְיָ, אֱלֹהֵינוּ מֶלֶךְ הָעוֹלָם,
בּוֹרֵא, פְּרִי הַגָּפֶן.

Boruch ato Adōnoy, Elōhaynu melech ho-ōlom,
bōray pree ha- gofen.

Praised be Thou, O Lord our God, King of the universe,
Who createst the fruit of the vine.

All drink the second cup of wine.

Preparing for the Meal

All the participants wash their hands, as was done earlier in the Seder, except this time, since a meal is to be eaten, the following blessing is recited:

בָּרוּךְ אַתָּה יְיָ, אֱלֹהֵינוּ מֶלֶךְ הָעוֹלָם, אֲשֶׁר
קִדְּשָׁנוּ בְּמִצְוֹתָיו, וְצִוָּנוּ עַל־נְטִילַת יָדַיִם.

Boruch ato Adōnoy Elōhaynu melech ho-olom, asher ki-d'shonu
b'mitzvōsov v'tzeevonu al n'teelas yo-do-yim.

Praised be Thou, O Lord our God, King of the universe, Who has sanctified us by His commandments, and commanded us concerning the laws of cleanliness.

מוֹצִיא · מַצָּה

The leader breaks pieces of the uppermost *matzo*, and also pieces of the remaining portion of the middle *matzo*, and distributes a portion to each participant. The following benedictions are recited before eating the *matzo*:

בָּרוּךְ אַתָּה יְיָ, אֱלֹהֵינוּ מֶלֶךְ הָעוֹלָם,
הַמּוֹצִיא לֶחֶם מִן־הָאָרֶץ.

Boruch ato Adōnoy Elōhaynu melech ho-ōlom, ha-mōtzee lechem min ho-oretz.

Praised be Thou, O Lord our God, King of the universe, Who brings forth bread from the earth.

בָּרוּךְ אַתָּה יְיָ, אֱלֹהֵינוּ מֶלֶךְ הָעוֹלָם, אֲשֶׁר
קִדְּשָׁנוּ בְּמִצְוֹתָיו, וְצִוָּנוּ עַל־אֲכִילַת מַצָּה.

Boruch ato Adōnoy Elōhaynu melech ho-ōlom, asher ki-d'shonu b'mitzvōsov v'tzeevonu al acheelas matzo.

Praised be Thou, O Lord our God, King of the universe, Who has sanctified us by His commandments, and commanded us to eat unleavened bread.

Those who have a pillow at their side eat the *matzo* in a reclining position as a sign of the freedom which this night emphasizes.

Bitter Herbs (Moror)

The leader places some horseradish and some *charoses* on the spoon of each participant. This is the ritual referred to in the Four Questions — "Why, on this night do we *dip* twice?" (The first dipping was the *karpas* (vegetable) in salt water.) The bitter herbs is a reminder of the bitter fate of the Israelites in Egypt. The *charoses* is symbolic of the mortar, or clay, out of which the Israelites made bricks for Pharaoh.

After each participant has received his portion, the following benediction is recited:

בָּרוּךְ אַתָּה יְיָ, אֱלֹהֵינוּ מֶלֶךְ הָעוֹלָם, אֲשֶׁר קִדְּשָׁנוּ בְּמִצְוֹתָיו, וְצִוָּנוּ עַל אֲכִילַת מָרוֹר.

Boruch ato Adōnoy Elōhaynu melech ho-ōlom, asher ki-d'shonu b'mitzvōsov v'tzeevonu al acheelas morōr.

Praised be Thou, O Lord our God, King of the universe, Who has sanctified us by His commandments, and commanded us to eat bitter herbs.

Hillel's Sandwich

Although the following selection refers to a sandwich made up of *pesach, matzo* and *moror,* we do not use the *pesach* (lamb) which applied only when the sacrificial system was in vogue during Temple days. Hillel, sometimes referred to as Hillel the First, or Hillel the Elder, was born in Babylonia about 75 B.C.E. In his youth, he left to study in Jerusalem. The Second Temple was still standing in his lifetime, and the sacrificial, paschal lamb was offered regularly on the altar during Passover. It is, therefore, understandable why Hillel would use a portion of the paschal lamb in the sandwich which he innovated.

In some households, it is customary to place *charoses,* in addition to the *moror,* between the two pieces of *matzo.*

זֵכֶר לְמִקְדָּשׁ כְּהִלֵּל. כֵּן עָשָׂה הַלֵּל,
בִּזְמַן שֶׁבֵּית הַמִּקְדָּשׁ הָיָה קַיָּם. הָיָה כּוֹרֵךְ
מַצָּה וּמָרוֹר וְאוֹכֵל בְּיַחַד. לְקַיֵּם מַה
שֶׁנֶּאֱמַר: עַל מַצּוֹת וּמְרוֹרִים יֹאכְלֻהוּ.

Such was the practice of Hillel the Great in the days when the Temple stood on its holy mountain in Jerusalem: he would take a piece of the paschal lamb, some *morōr,* and some *matzo,* and eat them together. Thus did he emphasize the true significance of the holiday of freedom, in fulfillment of the biblical injunction: "They shall eat the paschal lamb with unleavened bread and bitter herbs."

> The Seder platter is removed and a hard-boiled egg is served to each of the participants. The egg symbolizes the *korban chagigo,* which was the usual holiday sacrifice, offered regularly in the Temple. After the destruction of the second Temple (70 C.E.), roasted meat on the bone and a roasted egg were the two main courses at the festive Passover banquet. These were served as reminders of the original sacrifices offered in the Temple (the *korban pesach* and the *korban chagigo*). The egg is dipped in salt water and eaten. Salt water was a dish commonly used in oriental countries. For more information concerning the significance of the egg, consult the introductory section: "The Seder Table and Its Symbols."

שֻׁלְחָן עוֹרֵךְ

Dinner Is Served (Shulchon Oraych)

At this point the table is cleared. The Seder tray and the symbolic foods are removed, and the full meal is served.

The Hidden Matzo (Tzofun)

After the meal is concluded the leader searches for the *Afikomon*. When it is located (or ransomed) a small piece is distributed to each participant. The wine goblets are filled, and we are ready to recite the Grace After Meals.

The Jews of Morocco eat a piece of their *afikomon* and save the balance. They keep this piece of *matzo* as a good luck charm. They are confident that, in their travels, it will protect them against all danger. If a storm develops while they are on an ocean voyage, they throw the *matzo* into the raging sea, claiming that it has the power to calm the angry waters.

Many East European Jews, and their descendants, follow the custom of saving a piece of the *afikomon*. They tuck it away in a drawer, and leave it there until the next Passover, a year later, when it is replaced with a new piece. This custom developed in commemoration of the verse in Deuteronomy (16:13), "that thou mayest remember the day when thou camest forth out of the land of Egypt *all the days* of thy life."

WHERE, O WHERE SHALL WE HIDE THE AFIKOMON?

THE SEAT OF HONOR
and
THE MATZO OF HOPE

As a tangible expression of our concern for the plight of Soviet Jewry, and for the condition of the oppressed and persecuted in every corner of the modern world, we now place one more chair at our Seder table. Before this Seat of Honor we place a full table setting, and on the plate we place one whole *matzo* which we call the Matzo of Hope. In Israel, the custom has developed to place upon the Seat of Honor a large, hand-printed card, or a commercially prepared poster, which declares our commitment to work, unceasingly, towards the day when Jews, so desiring, will be permitted to leave the Soviet Union at will, as guaranteed by the charter of the United Nations.

Recite in unison:

This Seat of Honor and this Matzo of Hope that we have added to our table—why are they here? They are here to remind us that although 35 centuries have passed since the Pharaohs conspired to destroy the Jewish people, enlightened and scientifically sophisticated nations like the Union of Soviet Socialist Republics have not yet learned the lesson of history; they have not learned that no human being may be denied his liberty; that no community of people can be kept in physical or spiritual servitude, nor denied its right to free speech and free movement.

On this night of Passover, sitting here as free people at our Pesach Seder, we express our oneness with our fellow Jews in the Soviet Union. We understand their plight and we are concerned with their fate. In whatever way we are able, we shall, as individuals and as members of the community, work diligently and sincerely towards winning their complete and unbridled freedom. "Let my people go" will be our battle cry today as it was in the days of Moses and Aaron. We shall not rest, we shall not be at ease until all our people—and all mankind, everywhere—shall be fully free.

Grace After Meals (Boraych)

On Sabbath and festivals, Grace After Meals is introduced
by reading or chanting Psalm 126.

שִׁיר הַמַּעֲלוֹת

שִׁיר הַמַּעֲלוֹת.

בְּשׁוּב יְיָ אֶת־שִׁיבַת צִיּוֹן הָיִינוּ כְּחֹלְמִים.

אָז יִמָּלֵא שְׂחוֹק פִּינוּ וּלְשׁוֹנֵנוּ רִנָּה.

אָז יֹאמְרוּ בַגּוֹיִם הִגְדִּיל יְיָ לַעֲשׂוֹת עִם־אֵלֶּה.

הִגְדִּיל יְיָ לַעֲשׂוֹת עִמָּנוּ הָיִינוּ שְׂמֵחִים.

שׁוּבָה יְיָ אֶת־שְׁבִיתֵנוּ כַּאֲפִיקִים בַּנֶּגֶב.

הַזֹּרְעִים בְּדִמְעָה בְּרִנָּה יִקְצֹרוּ.

הָלוֹךְ יֵלֵךְ וּבָכֹה נֹשֵׂא מֶשֶׁךְ־הַזָּרַע,

בֹּא יָבֹא בְרִנָּה נֹשֵׂא אֲלֻמֹּתָיו.

TRANSLITERATION OF PSALM 126

Shir ha-ma-alōs, b'shuv Adōnoy es sheevas Tzee-yōn,
ho-yeenu k'chōl-mim

Oz yee-molay s'chōk peenu, u'l'shō'naynu reeno.

Oz yōmru va-gō-yim, hig-deel Adōnoy la-asōs im ayleh;
hig-deel Adōnoy la-asōs eemonu, ho-yeenu s'may-chim.

Shuvo Adōnoy es shvee-saynu, ka-afeekim ba-negev.

Ha-zōr'im b'dim-o, b'reeno yik-tzō-ru.

Ho-lōch yay-laych, u-vochō, nōsay meshech ha-zora.

Bō yovō v'reeno, nōsay a-lu-mōsov.

PSALM 126

When the Lord repatriated
The exiled of Zion,
We were as in a dream.
Laughter filled our mouths;
Mirth rolled off our tongues.
Then it was said among the nations:
"God did great things for them."
True, the Lord did great things for us,
And we were happy.
Restore, O Lord, our fortunes
Like the streams of the Negev;
For they who plant with tears,
Will surely reap in joy.

Leader:

רַבּוֹתַי נְבָרֵךְ.

Participants:

יְהִי שֵׁם יְיָ מְבֹרָךְ מֵעַתָּה וְעַד עוֹלָם.

Leader:

בִּרְשׁוּת רַבּוֹתַי נְבָרֵךְ [אֱלֹהֵינוּ] שֶׁאָכַלְנוּ מִשֶּׁלּוֹ.

Participants:

בָּרוּךְ [אֱלֹהֵינוּ] שֶׁאָכַלְנוּ מִשֶּׁלּוֹ וּבְטוּבוֹ חָיִינוּ.

All participants continue in unison:

בָּרוּךְ: אַתָּה יְיָ אֱלֹהֵינוּ מֶלֶךְ הָעוֹלָם, הַזָּן אֶת הָעוֹלָם
כֻּלּוֹ בְּטוּבוֹ, בְּחֵן בְּחֶסֶד וּבְרַחֲמִים, הוּא נוֹתֵן לֶחֶם לְכָל
בָּשָׂר, כִּי לְעוֹלָם חַסְדּוֹ. וּבְטוּבוֹ הַגָּדוֹל תָּמִיד לֹא חָסַר
לָנוּ וְאַל יֶחְסַר לָנוּ מָזוֹן לְעוֹלָם וָעֶד, בַּעֲבוּר שְׁמוֹ הַגָּדוֹל.
כִּי הוּא אֵל זָן וּמְפַרְנֵס לַכֹּל, וּמֵטִיב לַכֹּל, וּמֵכִין מָזוֹן לְכָל
בְּרִיּוֹתָיו אֲשֶׁר בָּרָא. בָּרוּךְ אַתָּה יְיָ, הַזָּן אֶת הַכֹּל.

Praised be Thou, O Lord
King of the universe,
Who provideth food for all;
Whose abundance and goodness
And mercy, endure forever.
Blessed art Thou, O Lord,
Sustainer of all mankind.

Assembly chants in unison:

Boruch ato Adōnoy, hazon es ha-kōl.

67

נוֹדֶה לְךָ יְיָ אֱלֹהֵינוּ עַל שֶׁהִנְחַלְתָּ לַאֲבוֹתֵינוּ אֶרֶץ חֶמְדָּה
טוֹבָה וּרְחָבָה, וְעַל שֶׁהוֹצֵאתָנוּ יְיָ אֱלֹהֵינוּ מֵאֶרֶץ מִצְרַיִם
וּפְדִיתָנוּ מִבֵּית עֲבָדִים, וְעַל בְּרִיתְךָ שֶׁחָתַמְתָּ בִּבְשָׂרֵנוּ,
וְעַל תּוֹרָתְךָ שֶׁלִּמַּדְתָּנוּ, וְעַל חֻקֶּיךָ שֶׁהוֹדַעְתָּנוּ, וְעַל חַיִּים
חֵן וָחֶסֶד שֶׁחוֹנַנְתָּנוּ, וְעַל אֲכִילַת מָזוֹן שֶׁאַתָּה זָן וּמְפַרְנֵס
אוֹתָנוּ תָּמִיד, בְּכָל יוֹם וּבְכָל עֵת וּבְכָל שָׁעָה.

WE RENDER THANKS

All read in unison:

We render thanks to Thee,
O Lord, our God.
For the desirable heritage
Thou has bequeathed unto us;
For having been released from bondage,
And for having been favored
With Thy Torah and Law.
And we thank Thee, too,
For the life of grace and kindness,
That Thou has bestowed upon us.

Assembly chants in unison:

B'chol yōm u-v'chol ays u-v'chol sho-o.

וְעַל הַכֹּל יְיָ אֱלֹהֵינוּ אֲנַחְנוּ מוֹדִים לָךְ וּמְבָרְכִים אוֹתָךְ,
יִתְבָּרַךְ שִׁמְךָ בְּפִי כָּל חַי תָּמִיד לְעוֹלָם וָעֶד, כַּכָּתוּב:
וְאָכַלְתָּ וְשָׂבָעְתָּ וּבֵרַכְתָּ אֶת יְיָ אֱלֹהֶיךָ עַל הָאָרֶץ הַטֹּבָה
אֲשֶׁר נָתַן לָךְ. בָּרוּךְ אַתָּה יְיָ, עַל הָאָרֶץ וְעַל הַמָּזוֹן.

FOR ALL THY GOODNESS

All read in unison:

For all Thy goodness
We thank Thee, O Lord,
And sing praises unto Thee.
May Thy glorious name,

Ever be on the lips
Of all living creatures.
As it is written:
"Thou shalt eat and be satisfied;
Then shalt thou bless the Lord thy God
For the good earth that he has bequeathed unto us."

Assembly chants in unison:

Ka-kosuv: V'ochalto, v'sovoto, u-vay-rachto es Adōnoy Elō-hecho al ho-oretz ha-tōvo asher nosan loch. Boruch ato Adōnoy al ho-oretz v'al ha-mozōn.

רַחֵם יְיָ אֱלֹהֵינוּ עַל יִשְׂרָאֵל עַמֶּךָ, וְעַל יְרוּשָׁלַיִם עִירֶךָ,
וְעַל צִיּוֹן מִשְׁכַּן כְּבוֹדֶךָ, וְעַל מַלְכוּת בֵּית דָּוִד מְשִׁיחֶךָ,
וְעַל הַבַּיִת הַגָּדוֹל וְהַקָּדוֹשׁ שֶׁנִּקְרָא שִׁמְךָ עָלָיו. אֱלֹהֵינוּ,
אָבִינוּ, רְעֵנוּ, זוּנֵנוּ, פַּרְנְסֵנוּ וְכַלְכְּלֵנוּ, וְהַרְוִיחֵנוּ,וְהַרְוַח לָנוּ,
יְיָ אֱלֹהֵינוּ, מְהֵרָה מִכָּל צָרוֹתֵינוּ. וְנָא אַל תַּצְרִיכֵנוּ, יְיָ
אֱלֹהֵינוּ, לֹא לִידֵי מַתְּנַת בָּשָׂר וָדָם וְלֹא לִידֵי הַלְוָאָתָם, כִּי
אִם לְיָדְךָ הַמְּלֵאָה, הַפְּתוּחָה, הַקְּדוֹשָׁה וְהָרְחָבָה, שֶׁלֹּא
נֵבוֹשׁ וְלֹא נִכָּלֵם לְעוֹלָם וָעֶד.

רְצֵה וְהַחֲלִיצֵנוּ, יְיָ אֱלֹהֵינוּ, בְּמִצְוֹתֶיךָ וּבְמִצְוַת יוֹם
הַשְּׁבִיעִי, הַשַּׁבָּת הַגָּדוֹל וְהַקָּדוֹשׁ הַזֶּה, כִּי יוֹם זֶה גָּדוֹל
וְקָדוֹשׁ הוּא לְפָנֶיךָ לִשְׁבָּת בּוֹ וְלָנוּחַ בּוֹ בְּאַהֲבָה, כְּמִצְוַת
רְצוֹנֶךָ. וּבִרְצוֹנְךָ הָנַח לָנוּ, יְיָ אֱלֹהֵינוּ, שֶׁלֹּא תְהִי צָרָה וְיָגוֹן
וַאֲנָחָה בְּיוֹם מְנוּחָתֵנוּ. וְהַרְאֵנוּ, יְיָ אֱלֹהֵינוּ, בְּנֶחָמַת צִיּוֹן
עִירֶךָ וּבְבִנְיַן יְרוּשָׁלַיִם עִיר קָדְשֶׁךָ, כִּי אַתָּה הוּא בַּעַל
הַיְשׁוּעוֹת וּבַעַל הַנֶּחָמוֹת.

אֱלֹהֵינוּ וֵאלֹהֵי אֲבוֹתֵינוּ, יַעֲלֶה וְיָבֹא וְיַגִּיעַ וְיֵרָאֶה
וְיֵרָצֶה וְיִשָּׁמַע, וְיִפָּקֵד וְיִזָּכֵר זִכְרוֹנֵנוּ וּפִקְדוֹנֵנוּ וְזִכְרוֹן
אֲבוֹתֵינוּ, וְזִכְרוֹן מָשִׁיחַ בֶּן דָּוִד עַבְדֶּךָ, וְזִכְרוֹן יְרוּשָׁלַיִם
עִיר קָדְשֶׁךָ, וְזִכְרוֹן כָּל עַמְּךָ בֵּית יִשְׂרָאֵל לְפָנֶיךָ לִפְלֵיטָה,
לְטוֹבָה, לְחֵן וּלְחֶסֶד וּלְרַחֲמִים, לְחַיִּים וּלְשָׁלוֹם בְּיוֹם חַג
הַמַּצּוֹת הַזֶּה. זָכְרֵנוּ, יְיָ אֱלֹהֵינוּ, בּוֹ לְטוֹבָה, וּפָקְדֵנוּ בּוֹ
לִבְרָכָה, וְהוֹשִׁיעֵנוּ בּוֹ לְחַיִּים. וּבִדְבַר יְשׁוּעָה וְרַחֲמִים חוּס
וְחָנֵּנוּ וְרַחֵם עָלֵינוּ וְהוֹשִׁיעֵנוּ, כִּי אֵלֶיךָ עֵינֵינוּ, כִּי אֵל מֶלֶךְ
חַנּוּן וְרַחוּם אָתָּה.

וּבְנֵה יְרוּשָׁלַיִם עִיר הַקֹּדֶשׁ בִּמְהֵרָה בְיָמֵינוּ. בָּרוּךְ אַתָּה
יְיָ, בּוֹנֵה בְרַחֲמָיו יְרוּשָׁלַיִם, אָמֵן.

70

בָּרוּךְ אַתָּה יְיָ אֱלֹהֵינוּ מֶלֶךְ הָעוֹלָם, הָאֵל אָבִינוּ מַלְכֵּנוּ,
אַדִּירֵנוּ בּוֹרְאֵנוּ גּוֹאֲלֵנוּ, יוֹצְרֵנוּ קְדוֹשֵׁנוּ קְדוֹשׁ יַעֲקֹב, רוֹעֵנוּ
רוֹעֵה יִשְׂרָאֵל, הַמֶּלֶךְ הַטּוֹב וְהַמֵּטִיב לַכֹּל, שֶׁבְּכָל יוֹם
וָיוֹם הוּא הֵטִיב, הוּא מֵטִיב, הוּא יֵיטִיב לָנוּ. הוּא גְמָלָנוּ,
הוּא גוֹמְלֵנוּ, הוּא יִגְמְלֵנוּ לָעַד, לְחֵן וּלְחֶסֶד וּלְרַחֲמִים
וּלְרֶוַח הַצָּלָה וְהַצְלָחָה, בְּרָכָה וִישׁוּעָה, נֶחָמָה, פַּרְנָסָה
וְכַלְכָּלָה, וְרַחֲמִים וְחַיִּים וְשָׁלוֹם וְכָל טוֹב, וּמִכָּל טוּב
לְעוֹלָם אַל יְחַסְּרֵנוּ.

הָרַחֲמָן

הָרַחֲמָן הוּא יִמְלֹךְ עָלֵינוּ לְעוֹלָם וָעֶד.

הָרַחֲמָן הוּא יִתְבָּרַךְ בַּשָּׁמַיִם וּבָאָרֶץ.

הָרַחֲמָן הוּא יִשְׁתַּבַּח לְדוֹר דּוֹרִים, וְיִתְפָּאַר בָּנוּ לָנֶצַח
נְצָחִים, וְיִתְהַדַּר בָּנוּ לָעַד וּלְעוֹלְמֵי עוֹלָמִים.

הָרַחֲמָן הוּא יְפַרְנְסֵנוּ בְּכָבוֹד.

הָרַחֲמָן הוּא יִשְׁבּוֹר עֻלֵּנוּ מֵעַל צַוָּארֵנוּ וְהוּא יוֹלִיכֵנוּ
קוֹמְמִיּוּת לְאַרְצֵנוּ.

הָרַחֲמָן הוּא יִשְׁלַח לָנוּ בְּרָכָה מְרֻבָּה בַּבַּיִת הַזֶּה וְעַל
שֻׁלְחָן זֶה שֶׁאָכַלְנוּ עָלָיו.

הָרַחֲמָן הוּא יִשְׁלַח לָנוּ אֶת אֵלִיָּהוּ הַנָּבִיא זָכוּר לַטּוֹב,
וִיבַשֶּׂר לָנוּ בְּשׂוֹרוֹת טוֹבוֹת, יְשׁוּעוֹת וְנֶחָמוֹת.

71

הָרַחֲמָן הוּא יְבָרֵךְ אֶת בַּעַל הַבַּיִת הַזֶּה, וְאֶת כָּל הַמְסֻבִּין, אוֹתָנוּ וְאֶת כָּל אֲשֶׁר לָנוּ. כְּמוֹ שֶׁנִּתְבָּרְכוּ אֲבוֹתֵינוּ אַבְרָהָם יִצְחָק וְיַעֲקֹב בַּכֹּל, מִכֹּל, כֹּל, כֵּן יְבָרֵךְ אוֹתָנוּ כֻּלָּנוּ יַחַד בִּבְרָכָה שְׁלֵמָה, וְנֹאמַר אָמֵן.

MAY THE LORD BLESS US

To be read responsively:

May the Lord rule over us forever.

May the Lord be blessed in heaven
   as He is on earth.

May the Lord be praised for all times;

May He find glory and honor, through us, eternally.

May the Lord sustain us with honor;

May the Lord sever from us all bonds of servitude,
   and lead us in pride to the land of promise.

May the Lord send His blessing to this household,
   and all who have joined us at this table.

בַּמָּרוֹם יְלַמְּדוּ (עֲלֵיהֶם וְ)עָלֵינוּ זְכוּת שֶׁתְּהִי לְמִשְׁמֶרֶת שָׁלוֹם, וְנִשָּׂא בְרָכָה מֵאֵת יְיָ וּצְדָקָה מֵאֱלֹהֵי יִשְׁעֵנוּ, וְנִמְצָא חֵן וְשֵׂכֶל טוֹב בְּעֵינֵי אֱלֹהִים וְאָדָם.

On Sabbath add:

הָרַחֲמָן הוּא יַנְחִילֵנוּ לְיוֹם שֶׁכֻּלּוֹ שַׁבָּת וּמְנוּחָה, לְחַיֵּי הָעוֹלָמִים.

הָרַחֲמָן הוּא יַנְחִילֵנוּ   יוֹם שֶׁכֻּלּוֹ טוֹב.

הָרַחֲמָן הוּא יְזַכֵּנוּ לִימוֹת הַמָּשִׁיחַ וּלְחַיֵּי הָעוֹלָם הַבָּא.

72

מִגְדּוֹל יְשׁוּעוֹת מַלְכּוֹ וְעֹשֶׂה חֶסֶד לִמְשִׁיחוֹ, לְדָוִד וּלְזַרְעוֹ
עַד עוֹלָם. עֹשֶׂה שָׁלוֹם בִּמְרוֹמָיו הוּא יַעֲשֶׂה שָׁלוֹם עָלֵינוּ
וְעַל כָּל יִשְׂרָאֵל, וְאִמְרוּ אָמֵן.

WORSHIP THE LORD IN REVERENCE

All read in unison:

Worship the Lord in reverence,
For his subjects know no want.
Give thanks to the Lord,
For His mercy endures forever.
Blessed art they who trust in the Lord,
The Lord will never forsake them.
May the Lord give strength unto His people
May He bless His people with peace. Amen.

יְראוּ אֶת יְיָ קְדֹשָׁיו, כִּי אֵין מַחְסוֹר לִירֵאָיו. כְּפִירִים
רָשׁוּ וְרָעֵבוּ, וְדֹרְשֵׁי יְיָ לֹא יַחְסְרוּ כָל טוֹב. הוֹדוּ לַיְיָ כִּי
טוֹב, כִּי לְעוֹלָם חַסְדּוֹ. פּוֹתֵחַ אֶת יָדֶךָ וּמַשְׂבִּיעַ לְכָל חַי
רָצוֹן. בָּרוּךְ הַגֶּבֶר אֲשֶׁר יִבְטַח בַּיְיָ, וְהָיָה יְיָ מִבְטַחוֹ. נַעַר
הָיִיתִי, גַם זָקַנְתִּי, וְלֹא רָאִיתִי צַדִּיק נֶעֱזָב וְזַרְעוֹ מְבַקֶּשׁ
לָחֶם. יְיָ עֹז לְעַמּוֹ יִתֵּן, יְיָ יְבָרֵךְ אֶת עַמּוֹ בַשָּׁלוֹם.

73

בָּרוּךְ אַתָּה יְיָ, אֱלֹהֵינוּ מֶלֶךְ הָעוֹלָם,
בּוֹרֵא, פְּרִי הַגָּפֶן.

Boruch ato Adōnoy, Elōhaynu melech ho-ōlom,
bōray pree ha- gofen.

Praised be Thou, O Lord our God, King of the universe,
Who createst the fruit of the vine.

After reciting the blessing, all drink the third cup of wine.

All the cups are again filled with wine for the fourth time.
The special cup of Elijah is also filled at this time.

ELIJAH AND THE OPEN DOOR

According to ancient Jewish tradition the prophet Elijah never
died, but merely vanished in heaven, having ascended there in
a fiery chariot drawn by fiery horses. The belief grew that, some-
day, Elijah would return to earth, and, as the forerunner of the
Messiah, he would prepare the way for a new, great age of peace
by resolving all disputes, and by preparing mankind for its
redemption.

Since Passover is the festival of freedom, it forever holds out
the hope of the redemption of mankind and deliverance from
all its ills. Who could be a more welcome guest than Elijah on
this festival of Passover? And so, in every Jewish home, a special cup is reserved for the "expected one," for the "guest of
honor."

The prayer that follows consists of verses from the Book of
Psalms and the Book of Lamentations. They were introduced
into the Haggadah during the Middle Ages when Jews suffered
severe hardships and merciless death at the hands of those who
professed to speak in the name of God, but whose actions be-
trayed this profession. Although Judaism does not condone vin-
dictiveness, as many statements in the Bible and Talmud attest
to, it does emphasize that the battle against evil and evil-doers
is a struggle that must be vigorously pursued, until a world of
equality and peace is established.

The door to the house, about to be opened, is a symbol of our
faith that the coming of a messianic age is not an impossible
dream. We, too, look for it, hope for it, and pray for it, as have
our ancestors for hundreds of generations before us.

74

שְׁפוֹךְ חֲמָתְךָ

שְׁפֹךְ חֲמָתְךָ אֶל הַגּוֹיִם, אֲשֶׁר לֹא יְדָעוּךָ
וְעַל מַמְלָכוֹת אֲשֶׁר בְּשִׁמְךָ, לֹא קָרָאוּ.
כִּי אָכַל אֶת יַעֲקֹב. וְאֶת נָוֵהוּ הֵשַׁמּוּ. שְׁפָךְ
עֲלֵיהֶם זַעְמֶךָ. וַחֲרוֹן אַפְּךָ, יַשִּׂיגֵם. תִּרְדֹּף
בְּאַף וְתַשְׁמִידֵם, מִתַּחַת שְׁמֵי יְיָ.

One participant leaves to open the front door of the house.

All rise and recite in unison:

May the wrath of the Almighty descend,
Upon all who know Him not.
Kingdoms and nations who betray Him,
Shall reap their inevitable lot.

May the wrath of the Lord descend,
Upon all who oppress and hate.
And all who trample the sacred,
This be their certain fate:

Thy fury and fire be upon them,
Who desecrate Thy delicate design!
Thy sting bring them low, dishonored;
Thy kingdom will yet shine.

אֵלִיָּהוּ הַנָּבִיא

אֵלִיָּהוּ הַתִּשְׁבִּי

אֵלִיָּהוּ, אֵלִיָּהוּ,   בִּמְהֵרָה בְיָמֵינוּ

אֵלִיָּהוּ הַגִּלְעָדִי.   יָבֹא אֵלֵינוּ.

עִם מָשִׁיחַ בֶּן־דָּוִד.

עִם מָשִׁיחַ בֶּן־דָּוִד.

"God does not decree that a man should be good or evil," said Moses Maimonides. "It is only fools and ignoramuses among Gentiles and Jews who maintain this nonsense. Every man is born free, to become as righteous as Moses or as wicked as Jeroboam; a student or an ignoramus; kind or cruel; generous or niggardly." It is, therefore, man himself who is responsible for the kind of life he builds. Man is the designer, the architect and the builder of his own fate.

All join in singing:

Elijah the Prophet, Elijah the Tishbite,
Elijah, Elijah, Elijah the Gileadite!
May he soon come,
Soon in our day,
With the Messiah — son of David.

ELIJAH THE TISHBITE.

"Do not think that in the Messianic Age anything will be changed in the world's order, or that some innovation will be introduced. Not at all! The world will continue in its normal course. The words of Isaiah (11:6): 'And the wolf shall dwell with the lamb, and the leopard shall lie down with the kid,' are to be understood as an allegory, meaning that Israel will live in peace with the wicked among the pagans. All of them will adopt the true faith and will never again steal or destroy. They will obey the commandments and will live peacefully with Israel."

MOSES MAIMONIDES

FOR THESE DO I WEEP!

We Remember

All rise, and the leader of the Seder recites the following:

On this Seder night we remember with tenderness the millions of our own people, and those of all nationalities and faiths, who only yesterday were mercilessly crushed by a tyrant more wicked than the Pharaoh who enslaved our fathers in Egypt. The blameless and the pure: men, women, children and babies did they annihilate in chambers of fire and in factories of death.

On this night of Passover we recall with pride the undaunted defenders of freedom in the ghettos of Europe—our brave brothers and sisters who defied the tyrant, even as did our ancestors in the days of Judah the Maccabee. They were the true defenders of man's dignity in their lifetime, and in their death they will not be forgotten. They bequeathed unto us an indelible legacy of courage.

We recall with love this evening, these and all martyrs of Jewish history who offered their bodies on the altar of faith—faith in the triumph of justice and the reign of brotherly love among all men.

ANI MAAMIN

If those assembled are familiar with the melody, all sing, *"Ani Maamin"*—"I Believe," the song of martyrs in the ghettos and liquidation camps of Europe during World War II.

I believe with perfect faith in the coming of the Messiah:
And though he tarry, none the less do I believe!

אֲנִי מַאֲמִין בֶּאֱמוּנָה שְׁלֵמָה בְּבִיאַת הַמָּשִׁיחַ, וְאַף עַל פִּי שֶׁיִּתְמַהְמֵהַּ, עִם כָּל זֶה אֲנִי מַאֲמִין.

All are seated.

"Dictators ride to and fro on tigers which they dare not dismount. And the tigers are getting hungry."

WINSTON S. CHURCHILL

"The Tree of Liberty must be refreshed, from time to time, with the blood of patriots and tyrants."

THOMAS JEFFERSON

PSALM 115 (Part I)

Psalm 115 is the third of the six psalms recited at the Seder service. The salvation of the Jewish people has been won, and now prayers of adoration to God, Who made it possible, are joyously spoken.

א לָנוּ יְיָ לֹא לָנוּ כִּי לְשִׁמְךָ תֵּן כָּבוֹד עַל חַסְדְּךָ עַל אֲמִתֶּךָ.

לָמָּה יֹאמְרוּ הַגּוֹיִם אַיֵּה נָא אֱלֹהֵיהֶם.

וֵאלֹהֵינוּ בַשָּׁמָיִם כֹּל אֲשֶׁר־חָפֵץ עָשָׂה.

עֲצַבֵּיהֶם כֶּסֶף וְזָהָב מַעֲשֵׂה יְדֵי אָדָם.

פֶּה־לָהֶם וְלֹא יְדַבֵּרוּ עֵינַיִם לָהֶם וְלֹא יִרְאוּ.

אָזְנַיִם לָהֶם וְלֹא יִשְׁמָעוּ אַף לָהֶם וְלֹא יְרִיחוּן.

יְדֵיהֶם וְלֹא יְמִישׁוּן רַגְלֵיהֶם וְלֹא יְהַלֵּכוּ.לֹא יֶהְגּוּ בִּגְרוֹנָם.

כְּמוֹהֶם יִהְיוּ עֹשֵׂיהֶם כֹּל אֲשֶׁר בֹּטֵחַ בָּהֶם.

יִשְׂרָאֵל בְּטַח בַּיְיָ עֶזְרָם וּמָגִנָּם הוּא.

בֵּית אַהֲרֹן בִּטְחוּ בַיְיָ עֶזְרָם וּמָגִנָּם הוּא.

יִרְאֵי יְיָ בִּטְחוּ בַיְיָ עֶזְרָם וּמָגִנָּם הוּא.

Responsive reading:

Not for our sakes, O Lord,
But for Thine, be kind to Thy faithful.

Why should the nations mockingly ask:
"Where is that God of theirs!"

We know that our God is in heaven,
All that He desires, He can do.

Their gods are made of silver and gold,
They are the works of man's hands.

They have mouths, but cannot speak,
They have eyes, but cannot see.

They have ears, but cannot hear,
They have nostrils, but cannot smell.

They have hands, but cannot feel,
They have feet, but cannot walk,
They have throats, but issue no sound.

As they are, so be their makers,
So be all who put their trust in them.

Let Israel put her trust in the Lord;
He is their Saviour and Protector.

Let the House of Aaron put their trust in the Lord;
He is their Saviour and Protector.

Let those who fear the Lord put their trust in Him;
He is their Saviour and Protector.

PSALM 115 (Part II)

The second half of Psalm 115 expresses the hope that God's blessings, so manifest during the period of the Exodus, will continue to be showered upon the whole household of Israel who trust in Him.

יְיָ זְכָרָנוּ יְבָרֵךְ יְבָרֵךְ אֶת בֵּית יִשְׂרָאֵל יְבָרֵךְ
אֶת בֵּית אַהֲרֹן.

יְבָרֵךְ יִרְאֵי יְיָ הַקְּטַנִּים עִם הַגְּדֹלִים.

יֹסֵף יְיָ עֲלֵיכֶם עֲלֵיכֶם וְעַל בְּנֵיכֶם.

בְּרוּכִים אַתֶּם לַיְיָ עֹשֵׂה שָׁמַיִם וָאָרֶץ.

הַשָּׁמַיִם שָׁמַיִם לַיְיָ וְהָאָרֶץ נָתַן לִבְנֵי אָדָם.

לֹא הַמֵּתִים יְהַלְלוּ יָהּ וְלֹא כָּל יֹרְדֵי דוּמָה.

וַאֲנַחְנוּ נְבָרֵךְ יָהּ מֵעַתָּה וְעַד עוֹלָם הַלְלוּיָהּ.

Participants read in unison:

The Lord is mindful of us!
May He bless the house of Israel,
May He bless the house of Aaron,
May He bless all who fear the Lord,
Children as well as grown-ups.

May the Lord multiply His blessings,
Upon you and upon your children.
Blessed are you before the Lord,
Creator of heaven and earth.

The heavens are the heavens of the Lord,
But the earth did He give for the children of man.

The dead cannot offer praise to the Lord,
Nor can they who go down in silence.

But we will praise the Lord, from this time
And forevermore, *Halleluyah!*

PSALM 116

Psalm 116 expresses the epitomy of personal faith. Confronted
by the defeats of life, the Psalmist keeps his faith in God with
the same degree of steadfastness as when he enjoyed life's
victories.

אָהַבְתִּי כִּי יִשְׁמַע יְיָ אֶת קוֹלִי תַּחֲנוּנָי.

כִּי הִטָּה אָזְנוֹ לִי וּבְיָמַי אֶקְרָא.

אֲפָפוּנִי חֶבְלֵי מָוֶת וּמְצָרֵי שְׁאוֹל מְצָאוּנִי צָרָה וְיָגוֹן אֶמְצָא.

וּבְשֵׁם יְיָ אֶקְרָא אָנָּה יְיָ מַלְּטָה נַפְשִׁי.

חַנּוּן יְיָ וְצַדִּיק וֵאלֹהֵינוּ מְרַחֵם.

שֹׁמֵר פְּתָאִים יְיָ דַּלֹּתִי וְלִי יְהוֹשִׁיעַ.

שׁוּבִי נַפְשִׁי לִמְנוּחָיְכִי כִּי יְיָ גָּמַל עָלָיְכִי.

כִּי חִלַּצְתָּ נַפְשִׁי מִמָּוֶת אֶת עֵינִי מִן דִּמְעָה אֶת רַגְלִי מִדָּחִי.

אֶתְהַלֵּךְ לִפְנֵי יְיָ בְּאַרְצוֹת הַחַיִּים.

הֶאֱמַנְתִּי כִּי אֲדַבֵּר אֲנִי עָנִיתִי מְאֹד.

אֲנִי אָמַרְתִּי בְחָפְזִי כָּל הָאָדָם כֹּזֵב.

To be read responsively:

I am pleased that God hears my voice,
That He listens to my cry of supplication.

Because He is attentive to my pleas,
I will call upon Him all my days.

Even when the cords of death surrounded me,
When the traps of the netherworld ensnared me,
And only sorrow and despair were my lot,
Even then did I call upon the Lord.

"Please, O Lord! Save my life!
For Thou art gracious and righteous."

Our God is truly merciful,
He is the guardian of the simple-minded.

Even when I was low, He raised me up.
My life is once again at peace.

The Lord dealt kindly with me,
He delivered me from death.

He removed all tears from my eyes,
And saved my feet from stumbling.

Once again shall I walk before the Lord
In the land of the living.

Even in my misery, when I once did say,
"All men are liars,"
Truly, I did believe in the Lord.

מָה אָשִׁיב לַיָי כָּל תַּגְמוּלֽוֹהִי עָלָי.

כּוֹס יְשׁוּעוֹת אֶשָּׂא וּבְשֵׁם יְיָ אֶקְרָא.

נְדָרַי לַיָי אֲשַׁלֵּם נֶגְדָה נָּא לְכָל עַמּוֹ.

יָקָר בְּעֵינֵי יְיָ הַמָּוְתָה לַחֲסִידָיו.

אָנָּה יְיָ כִּי אֲנִי עַבְדֶּךָ אֲנִי עַבְדְּךָ בֶּן־אֲמָתֶךָ פִּתַּחְתָּ לְמוֹסֵרָי.

לְךָ אֶזְבַּח זֶבַח תּוֹדָה וּבְשֵׁם יְיָ אֶקְרָא.

נְדָרַי לַיָי אֲשַׁלֵּם נֶגְדָה נָּא לְכָל עַמּוֹ.

בְּחַצְרוֹת בֵּית יְיָ בְּתוֹכֵכִי יְרוּשָׁלָיִם הַלְלוּיָהּ.

Leader:

> How can I repay the Lord,
> For all His goodness to me?
> I shall lift up the cup of thanksgiving
> And call upon the name of the Lord.
> I shall make good every vow to the Lord,
> In the presence of all His people.

Participants:

> Before Thee, O Lord, will I offer thanksgiving,
> And I will call upon Thy name,
> In the presence of all Thy people,
> In the courts of Thy House,
> In the midst of Jerusalem. Halleluyah!

Psalm 117

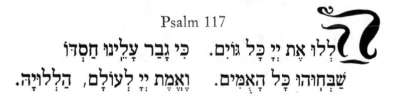

הַלְלוּ אֶת יְיָ כָּל גּוֹיִם. כִּי גָבַר עָלֵינוּ חַסְדּוֹ
שַׁבְּחוּהוּ כָּל הָאֻמִּים. וֶאֱמֶת יְיָ לְעוֹלָם, הַלְלוּיָהּ.

84

PSALM 117

To be read in unison:

Praise the Lord, all you nations,
Laud Him all you people.
Great is His love for us,
Everlasting is His faithfulness. Halleluyah!

הוֹדוּ לַיְיָ כִּי טוֹב   כִּי לְעוֹלָם חַסְדּוֹ.

יֹאמַר נָא יִשְׂרָאֵל   כִּי לְעוֹלָם חַסְדּוֹ.

יֹאמְרוּ נָא בֵית־אַהֲרֹן   כִּי לְעוֹלָם חַסְדּוֹ.

יֹאמְרוּ נָא יִרְאֵי יְיָ   כִּי לְעוֹלָם חַסְדּוֹ.

PSALM 118

Leader: Give thanks to the Lord, for He is good;
His love is everlasting.
Let Israel proclaim:

Participants: His love is everlasting.

85

Leader:	Let the House of Aaron proclaim:
Participants:	His love is everlasting.
Leader:	Let the Lord's faithful proclaim:
Participants:	His love is everlasting.

To be read responsively:

מִן הַמֵּצַר קָרָאתִי יָּה עָנָנִי בַמֶּרְחָב יָה.

יְיָ לִי לֹא אִירָא מַה יַּעֲשֶׂה לִי אָדָם.

יְיָ לִי בְּעֹזְרָי וַאֲנִי אֶרְאֶה בְשֹׂנְאָי.

טוֹב לַחֲסוֹת בַּיְיָ מִבְּטֹחַ בָּאָדָם.

טוֹב לַחֲסוֹת בַּיְיָ מִבְּטֹחַ בִּנְדִיבִים.

כָּל גּוֹיִם סְבָבוּנִי בְּשֵׁם יְיָ כִּי אֲמִילַם.

סַבּוּנִי גַם סְבָבוּנִי בְּשֵׁם יְיָ כִּי אֲמִילַם.

סַבּוּנִי כִדְבֹרִים דֹעֲכוּ כְּאֵשׁ קוֹצִים בְּשֵׁם יְיָ כִּי אֲמִילַם.

דָּחֹה דְחִיתַנִי לִנְפֹּל וַיְיָ עֲזָרָנִי.

עָזִּי וְזִמְרָת יָהּ וַיְהִי לִי לִישׁוּעָה.

קוֹל רִנָּה וִישׁוּעָה בְּאָהֳלֵי צַדִּיקִים יְמִין יְיָ עֹשָׂה חָיִל.

יְמִין יְיָ רוֹמֵמָה יְמִין יְיָ עֹשָׂה חָיִל.

לֹא אָמוּת כִּי אֶחְיֶה וַאֲסַפֵּר מַעֲשֵׂי יָהּ.

יַסֹּר יִסְּרַנִּי יָּהּ וְלַמָּוֶת לֹא נְתָנָנִי.

פִּתְחוּ לִי שַׁעֲרֵי צֶדֶק אָבֹא בָם אוֹדֶה יָהּ.

זֶה הַשַּׁעַר לַיְיָ צַדִּיקִים יָבֹאוּ בוֹ.

86

In my anguish
I called upon the Lord,
He answered me;
And set me free.

The Lord is with me,
I shall not fear.

What harm can anyone do to me,
When the Lord is with me?

It is better to trust in the Lord,
Than to trust in man;
It is better to trust in the Lord,
Than to trust in princes.

Even when surrounded by enemies on all sides—
In God's name,
I will surely overcome them.

Even when they swarm about me like bees—
In God's name,
I will surely overcome them;

They will collapse like straw afire.

Though they conspire to bring my downfall,
The Lord will help me.
The Lord is my strength and my song,
I shall triumph through Him.

The homes of the righteous
Resound with success,
The power of the Lord
Has produced victory.

Though the Lord did severely chastise me,
He did not doom me to death.

In My Anguish I Called Upon The Lord!

88

I shall not die; for I shall live
To proclaim the wonders of the Lord.

Open to me the gates of righteousness,
That I may enter and praise the Lord.

I will praise Thee, O Lord,
For Thou hast answered me;
Thou hast been my deliverer.

The stone which the builders rejected,
Has now become the chief cornerstone.

All this is the Lord's doing,
It is wonderful in our eyes.

This day, the Lord has made,
Let us rejoice and be glad in it.

Each of the following four verses is read twice:

אוֹדְךָ כִּי עֲנִיתָנִי וַתְּהִי לִי לִישׁוּעָה.

אֶבֶן מָאֲסוּ הַבּוֹנִים הָיְתָה לְרֹאשׁ פִּנָּה.

מֵאֵת יְיָ הָיְתָה זֹּאת הִיא נִפְלָאת בְּעֵינֵינוּ.

זֶה הַיּוֹם עָשָׂה יְיָ נָגִילָה וְנִשְׂמְחָה בוֹ.

נָא יְיָ הוֹשִׁיעָה נָּא.

אָנָּא יְיָ הוֹשִׁיעָה נָּא.

אָנָּא יְיָ הַצְלִיחָה נָא.

אָנָּא יְיָ הַצְלִיחָה נָא.

Each of the following four verses is read twice:

בָּרוּךְ הַבָּא בְּשֵׁם יְיָ בֵּרַכְנוּכֶם מִבֵּית יְיָ.

אֵל יְיָ וַיָּאֶר לָנוּ אִסְרוּ חַג בַּעֲבֹתִים עַד

קַרְנוֹת הַמִּזְבֵּחַ.

אֵלִי אַתָּה וְאוֹדֶךָ אֱלֹהַי אֲרוֹמְמֶךָּ.

הוֹדוּ לַיְיָ כִּי טוֹב כִּי לְעוֹלָם חַסְדוֹ.

יְהַלְלוּךָ יְיָ אֱלֹהֵינוּ כָּל מַעֲשֶׂיךָ. וַחֲסִידֶיךָ צַדִּיקִים עוֹשֵׂי רְצוֹנֶךָ. וְכָל
עַמְּךָ בֵּית יִשְׂרָאֵל בְּרִנָּה יוֹדוּ וִיבָרְכוּ וִישַׁבְּחוּ וִיפָאֲרוּ וִירוֹמְמוּ וְיַעֲרִיצוּ
וְיַקְדִּישׁוּ וְיַמְלִיכוּ אֶת שִׁמְךָ מַלְכֵּנוּ. כִּי לְךָ טוֹב לְהוֹדוֹת. וּלְשִׁמְךָ נָאֶה
לְזַמֵּר. כִּי מֵעוֹלָם וְעַד עוֹלָם אַתָּה אֵל.

הוֹדוּ

כִּי לְעוֹלָם חַסְדוֹ.	הוֹדוּ לַיְיָ כִּי טוֹב
כִּי לְעוֹלָם חַסְדוֹ.	הוֹדוּ לֵאלֹהֵי הָאֱלֹהִים
כִּי לְעוֹלָם חַסְדוֹ.	הוֹדוּ לַאֲדֹנֵי הָאֲדֹנִים
כִּי לְעוֹלָם חַסְדוֹ.	לְעֹשֵׂה נִפְלָאוֹת גְּדוֹלוֹת לְבַדּוֹ
כִּי לְעוֹלָם חַסְדוֹ.	לְעֹשֵׂה הַשָּׁמַיִם בִּתְבוּנָה
כִּי לְעוֹלָם חַסְדוֹ.	לְרוֹקַע הָאָרֶץ עַל הַמָּיִם
כִּי לְעוֹלָם חַסְדוֹ.	לְעֹשֵׂה אוֹרִים גְּדֹלִים
כִּי לְעוֹלָם חַסְדוֹ.	אֶת הַשֶּׁמֶשׁ לְמֶמְשֶׁלֶת בַּיוֹם
כִּי לְעוֹלָם חַסְדוֹ.	אֶת הַיָּרֵחַ וְכוֹכָבִים לְמֶמְשְׁלוֹת בַּלָּיְלָה
כִּי לְעוֹלָם חַסְדוֹ.	לְמַכֵּה מִצְרַיִם בִּבְכוֹרֵיהֶם

וַיּוֹצֵא יִשְׂרָאֵל מִתּוֹכָם	כִּי לְעוֹלָם חַסְדּוֹ.
בְּיָד חֲזָקָה וּבִזְרוֹעַ נְטוּיָה	כִּי לְעוֹלָם חַסְדּוֹ.
לְגֹזֵר יַם־סוּף לִגְזָרִים	כִּי לְעוֹלָם חַסְדּוֹ.
וְהֶעֱבִיר יִשְׂרָאֵל בְּתוֹכוֹ	כִּי לְעוֹלָם חַסְדּוֹ.
וְנִעֵר פַּרְעֹה וְחֵילוֹ בְיַם־סוּף	כִּי לְעוֹלָם חַסְדּוֹ.
לְמוֹלִיךְ עַמּוֹ בַּמִּדְבָּר	כִּי לְעוֹלָם חַסְדּוֹ.
לְמַכֵּה מְלָכִים גְּדוֹלִים	כִּי לְעוֹלָם חַסְדּוֹ.
וַיַּהֲרֹג מְלָכִים אַדִּירִים	כִּי לְעוֹלָם חַסְדּוֹ.
לְסִיחוֹן מֶלֶךְ הָאֱמֹרִי	כִּי לְעוֹלָם חַסְדּוֹ.
וּלְעוֹג מֶלֶךְ הַבָּשָׁן	כִּי לְעוֹלָם חַסְדּוֹ.
וְנָתַן אַרְצָם לְנַחֲלָה	כִּי לְעוֹלָם חַסְדּוֹ.
נַחֲלָה לְיִשְׂרָאֵל עַבְדּוֹ	כִּי לְעוֹלָם חַסְדּוֹ.
שֶׁבְּשִׁפְלֵנוּ זָכַר לָנוּ	כִּי לְעוֹלָם חַסְדּוֹ.
וַיִּפְרְקֵנוּ מִצָּרֵינוּ	כִּי לְעוֹלָם חַסְדּוֹ.
נֹתֵן לֶחֶם לְכָל בָּשָׂר	כִּי לְעוֹלָם חַסְדּוֹ.
הוֹדוּ לְאֵל הַשָּׁמָיִם	כִּי לְעוֹלָם חַסְדּוֹ.

The Soul of All Life (Nishmas)

The *Nishmas* prayer that follows is part of every Sabbath and festival service, when it is recited immediately after the Song of Moses (from Exodus 15). The Song of Moses is one of the most fiery, and vividly poetic, portions of the Bible. In it the Children of Israel relived the glorious and triumphant moments of the Exodus. Incorporated in it is the climactic verse of acclaim in which Moses and the Children of Israel sing:

> *Mee cho-mocho bo-aylim Adonoy*
> *Mee komocho ne-edor ba-kodesh*
> *Noro s'heelos, osay feleh.*

> Who is like unto Thee, O Lord
>   among thy mighty?
> Who is like unto Thee, exalted
>   in holiness?
> Thy wondrous deeds are shrouded
>   in awe!

Nishmas, which was composed in talmudic times, picks up this theme and expresses, with breathtaking beauty, heartfelt thankfulness for the life of freedom made possible by the Exodus.

שְׁמַת כָּל חַי תְּבָרֵךְ אֶת שִׁמְךָ יְיָ אֱלֹהֵינוּ. וְרוּחַ כָּל בָּשָׂר תְּפָאֵר וּתְרוֹמֵם זִכְרְךָ מַלְכֵּנוּ תָּמִיד. מִדְהָעוֹלָם וְעַד הָעוֹלָם אַתָּה אֵל. וּמִבַּלְעָדֶיךָ אֵין לָנוּ מֶלֶךְ גּוֹאֵל וּמוֹשִׁיעַ פּוֹדֶה וּמַצִּיל וּמְפַרְנֵס וּמְרַחֵם בְּכָל־עֵת צָרָה וְצוּקָה. אֵיךְדלָנוּ מֶלֶךְ אֶלָּא אָתָּה. אֱלֹהֵי הָרִאשׁוֹנִים וְהָאַחֲרוֹנִים. אֱלוֹהַּ כָּל בְּרִיּוֹת אֲדוֹן כָּל תּוֹלָדוֹת. הַמְהֻלָּל בְּרֹב הַתִּשְׁבָּחוֹת. הַמְנַהֵג עוֹלָמוֹ בְּחֶסֶד וּבְרִיּוֹתָיו בְּרַחֲמִים. וַיְיָ לֹא יָנוּם וְלֹא יִישָׁן. הַמְעוֹרֵר יְשֵׁנִים וְהַמֵּקִיץ נִרְדָּמִים וְהַמֵּשִׂיחַ אִלְּמִים וְהַמַּתִּיר אֲסוּרִים וְהַסּוֹמֵךְ נוֹפְלִים וְהַזּוֹקֵף כְּפוּפִים. לְךָ לְבַדְּךָ אֲנַחְנוּ מוֹדִים. אִלּוּ פִינוּ מָלֵא שִׁירָה כַיָּם וּלְשׁוֹנֵנוּ רִנָּה כַּהֲמוֹן גַּלָּיו וְשִׂפְתוֹתֵינוּ שֶׁבַח כְּמֶרְחֲבֵי

רָקִיעַ וְעֵינֵינוּ מְאִירוֹת כַּשֶּׁמֶשׁ וְכַיָּרֵחַ וְיָדֵינוּ פְרוּשׂוֹת כְּנִשְׁרֵי שָׁמַיִם וְרַגְלֵינוּ
קַלּוֹת כָּאַיָּלוֹת. אֵין אֲנַחְנוּ מַסְפִּיקִים לְהוֹדוֹת לְךָ יְיָ אֱלֹהֵינוּ וֵאלֹהֵי
אֲבוֹתֵינוּ וּלְבָרֵךְ אֶת שְׁמֶךָ עַל אַחַת מֵאֶלֶף אֶלֶף אַלְפֵי אֲלָפִים וְרִבֵּי
רְבָבוֹת פְּעָמִים הַטּוֹבוֹת שֶׁעָשִׂיתָ עִם אֲבוֹתֵינוּ וְעִמָּנוּ. מִמִּצְרַיִם גְּאַלְתָּנוּ
יְיָ אֱלֹהֵינוּ וּמִבֵּית עֲבָדִים פְּדִיתָנוּ. בְּרָעָב זַנְתָּנוּ וּבְשָׂבָע כִּלְכַּלְתָּנוּ.
וּמֵחֶרֶב הִצַּלְתָּנוּ וּמִדֶּבֶר מִלַּטְתָּנוּ. וּמֵחֳלָיִם רָעִים וְנֶאֱמָנִים דִּלִּיתָנוּ.
עַד הֵנָּה עֲזָרוּנוּ רַחֲמֶיךָ. וְלֹא עֲזָבוּנוּ חֲסָדֶיךָ. וְאַל תִּטְּשֵׁנוּ יְיָ אֱלֹהֵינוּ
לָנֶצַח. עַל כֵּן אֵבָרִים שֶׁפִּלַּגְתָּ בָּנוּ וְרוּחַ וּנְשָׁמָה שֶׁנָּפַחְתָּ בְּאַפֵּינוּ וְלָשׁוֹן
אֲשֶׁר שַׂמְתָּ בְּפִינוּ. הֵן הֵם יוֹדוּ וִיבָרְכוּ וִישַׁבְּחוּ וִיפָאֲרוּ וִירוֹמְמוּ וְיַעֲרִיצוּ
וְיַקְדִּישׁוּ וְיַמְלִיכוּ אֶת־שִׁמְךָ מַלְכֵּנוּ. כִּי כָל פֶּה לְךָ יוֹדֶה. וְכָל לָשׁוֹן
לְךָ תִשָּׁבַע. וְכָל בֶּרֶךְ לְךָ תִכְרַע. וְכָל קוֹמָה לְפָנֶיךָ תִשְׁתַּחֲוֶה. וְכָל
לְבָבוֹת יִירָאוּךָ. וְכָל קֶרֶב וּכְלָיוֹת יְזַמְּרוּ לִשְׁמֶךָ. כַּדָּבָר שֶׁכָּתוּב.
כָּל עַצְמוֹתַי תֹּאמַרְנָה יְיָ מִי כָמוֹךָ. מַצִּיל עָנִי מֵחָזָק מִמֶּנּוּ וְעָנִי וְאֶבְיוֹן
מִגֹּזְלוֹ. מִי יִדְמֶה לָּךְ וּמִי יִשְׁוֶה לָּךְ וּמִי יַעֲרָךְ לָךְ. הָאֵל הַגָּדוֹל הַגִּבּוֹר
וְהַנּוֹרָא אֵל עֶלְיוֹן קֹנֵה שָׁמַיִם וָאָרֶץ. נְהַלֶּלְךָ וּנְשַׁבֵּחֲךָ וּנְפָאֶרְךָ וּנְבָרֵךְ
אֶת שֵׁם קָדְשֶׁךָ. כָּאָמוּר לְדָוִד בָּרְכִי נַפְשִׁי אֶת יְיָ וְכָל קְרָבַי אֶת שֵׁם
קָדְשׁוֹ.

הָאֵל בְּתַעֲצֻמוֹת

הָאֵל בְּתַעֲצֻמוֹת עֻזֶּךָ. הַגָּדוֹל בִּכְבוֹד שְׁמֶךָ. הַגִּבּוֹר לָנֶצַח וְהַנּוֹרָא
בְּנוֹרְאוֹתֶיךָ. הַמֶּלֶךְ הַיּוֹשֵׁב עַל־כִּסֵּא רָם וְנִשָּׂא.

THE SOUL OF ALL LIFE

To be read responsively:

The soul of all life
Shall bless Thy name, O Lord.
The spirit breathed into every creature,
Bespeaks Thy glory and greatness.

We have no king, but Thee, O God,
No redeemer, but Thee alone.
For Thou alone art God,
From the very beginning to the end of time.

The Lord does not slumber,
Nor does He sleep.
He restores to life those who sleep;
He awakens those who slumber.

He restores speech to the speechless,
And removes the bonds of the captive.
He strengthens those who fall,
And straightens the backs of those who are stooped.

To Thee alone do we give thanks, O Lord.
To Thee alone are all praises due.
For we are fallible and fragile,
Full power to utter Thy praises fails us.

Were hymns of praise as flowing in our mouths
As the waters of the sea;
Were songs of joy to roll from our tongues
As the waves of the ocean;
Were psalms of praise to lay on our lips
As the spacious expanse of the heavens;
Were our eyes as bright and penetrating
As the light of the sun;

Were our hands as expansive
As the wings of the heavenly eagle;
And our feet as fleet
As the sprightly hind—
Then, even then, would it be impossible
To express in words or deeds
Our debt of gratitude to Thee
For the multitude of blessings and kindnesses
Thou hast bestowed upon us.

Thou hast redeemed us from Egypt, O Lord,
        Our God;
And hast freed us from the bondage of slavery.
Thou hast fed us in times of famine,
And hast saved us from raging plagues and illness.

For all Thy goodness and compassion
That alone has helped and saved us,
We owe Thee allegiance.

Limited though we are in power,
We shall use every organ at our command
To give Thee thanks and praise;
To exalt, glorify and extol Thy name.

Every mouth will thank Thee,
Every tongue will pledge Thee loyalty.
Before Thee, every knee will bend,
Every man will bow down,
And sing praises to Thy name:
"Lord, who is like unto Thee?
Who, like Thee, saves the poor from the oppressor,
The needy from those who would despoil him?"

For praise is becoming to Thee,
Songs of thankfulness worthy of Thee.
Praised be Thou, exalted God and King,
To Whom all praise is due.

שׁוֹכֵן עַד

וְכֵן עַד מָרוֹם וְקָדוֹשׁ שְׁמוֹ. וְכָתוּב. רַנְּנוּ צַדִּיקִים בַּיְיָ לַיְשָׁרִים נָאוָה
תְהִלָּה. בְּפִי יְשָׁרִים תִּתְהַלָּל. וּבְדִבְרֵי צַדִּיקִים תִּתְבָּרַךְ. וּבִלְשׁוֹן חֲסִידִים
תִּתְרוֹמָם. וּבְקֶרֶב קְדוֹשִׁים תִּתְקַדָּשׁ.

וּבְמַקְהֲלוֹת רִבְבוֹת עַמְּךָ בֵּית יִשְׂרָאֵל בְּרִנָּה יִתְפָּאַר שִׁמְךָ מַלְכֵּנוּ
בְּכָל דּוֹר וָדוֹר. שֶׁכֵּן חוֹבַת כָּל הַיְצוּרִים לְפָנֶיךָ יְיָ אֱלֹהֵינוּ וֵאלֹהֵי
אֲבוֹתֵינוּ. לְהוֹדוֹת לְהַלֵּל לְשַׁבֵּחַ לְפָאֵר לְרוֹמֵם לְהַדֵּר לְבָרֵךְ לְעַלֵּה
וּלְקַלֵּס עַל כָּל דִּבְרֵי שִׁירוֹת וְתִשְׁבְּחוֹת דָּוִד בֶּן יִשַׁי עַבְדְּךָ מְשִׁיחֶךָ.

יִשְׁתַּבַּח שִׁמְךָ לָעַד מַלְכֵּנוּ הָאֵל הַמֶּלֶךְ הַגָּדוֹל וְהַקָּדוֹשׁ בַּשָּׁמַיִם וּבָאָרֶץ.
כִּי לְךָ נָאֶה יְיָ אֱלֹהֵינוּ וֵאלֹהֵי אֲבוֹתֵינוּ שִׁיר וּשְׁבָחָה הַלֵּל וְזִמְרָה
עֹז וּמֶמְשָׁלָה נֶצַח גְּדֻלָּה וּגְבוּרָה תְּהִלָּה וְתִפְאֶרֶת קְדֻשָּׁה וּמַלְכוּת
בְּרָכוֹת וְהוֹדָאוֹת מֵעַתָּה וְעַד עוֹלָם.

בָּרוּךְ אַתָּה יְיָ אֵל מֶלֶךְ גָּדוֹל בַּתִּשְׁבָּחוֹת. אֵל הַהוֹדָאוֹת. אֲדוֹן הַנִּפְלָאוֹת.
הַבּוֹחֵר בְּשִׁירֵי זִמְרָה. מֶלֶךְ אֵל חֵי הָעוֹלָמִים.

THE FOURTH CUP OF WINE

בָּרוּךְ אַתָּה יְיָ, אֱלֹהֵינוּ מֶלֶךְ הָעוֹלָם,
בּוֹרֵא, פְּרִי הַגָּפֶן.

Boruch ato Adōnoy, Elōhaynu melech ho-ōlom,
bōray pree ha- gofen.

Praised be Thou, O Lord our God, King of the universe,
Who createst the fruit of the vine.

After reciting the blessing we partake of the fourth cup of wine.

רוּךְ אַתָּה יְיָ אֱלֹהֵינוּ מֶלֶךְ הָעוֹלָם. עַל הַגֶּפֶן וְעַל פְּרִי הַגֶּפֶן. וְעַל
תְּנוּבַת הַשָּׂדֶה וְעַל אֶרֶץ חֶמְדָּה טוֹבָה וּרְחָבָה שֶׁרָצִיתָ וְהִנְחַלְתָּ לַאֲבוֹתֵינוּ
לֶאֱכוֹל מִפִּרְיָהּ וְלִשְׂבּוֹעַ מִטּוּבָהּ. רַחֵם יְיָ אֱלֹהֵינוּ עַל יִשְׂרָאֵל עַמֶּךְ
וְעַל יְרוּשָׁלַיִם עִירָךְ. וְעַל צִיּוֹן מִשְׁכַּן כְּבוֹדֶךְ. וְעַל מִזְבַּחַךְ וְעַל הֵיכָלֶךְ.
וּבְנֵה יְרוּשָׁלַיִם עִיר הַקֹּדֶשׁ בִּמְהֵרָה בְיָמֵינוּ. וְהַעֲלֵנוּ לְתוֹכָהּ וְשַׂמְּחֵנוּ
בְּבִנְיָנָהּ. וְנֹאכַל מִפִּרְיָהּ וְנִשְׂבַּע מִטּוּבָהּ. וּנְבָרֶכְךָ עָלֶיהָ בִּקְדֻשָּׁה
וּבְטָהֳרָה. וּרְצֵה וְהַחֲלִיצֵנוּ בְּיוֹם הַשַּׁבָּת הַזֶּה] וְשַׂמְּחֵנוּ בְּיוֹם חַג הַמַּצּוֹת
הַזֶּה. כִּי אַתָּה יְיָ טוֹב וּמֵטִיב לַכֹּל וְנוֹדֶה לְּךָ עַל הָאָרֶץ וְעַל פְּרִי הַגֶּפֶן.
בָּרוּךְ אַתָּה יְיָ עַל הָאָרֶץ וְעַל פְּרִי הַגֶּפֶן.

We are grateful to Thee, O Lord, Our God, King of the universe, for the fruit of the vine which we have partaken of this night, and for the yield of the good earth which we have enjoyed. Thou hast blessed us, even as Thou hast blessed our ancestors of old, with a land, beautiful and bountiful, rich in yield and goodness.

May this Festival of Freedom infuse within us a new appreciation for all the blessings of mind and spirit which Thou has bestowed upon us.

Conclusion

The official portion of the Seder concludes with the following liturgical poem, composed by Rabbi Joseph Tov Elem in the 11th century:

חֲסַל סִדּוּר פֶּסַח כְּהִלְכָתוֹ

כְּכָל־מִשְׁפָּטוֹ וְחֻקָתוֹ

כַּאֲשֶׁר זָכִינוּ לְסַדֵּר אוֹתוֹ

כֵּן נִזְכֶּה לַעֲשׂוֹתוֹ.

זָךְ שׁוֹכֵן מְעוֹנָה

קוֹמֵם קְהַל עֲדַת מִי מָנָה

קָרֵב נַהֵל נִטְעֵי כַנָּה

פְּדוּיִם לְצִיּוֹן בְּרִנָּה.

All read in unison:

The rites of the Seder are now concluded, in
　　accordance with ancient precept and custom.

With the same zeal that we have prepared for
　　this day,
May we plan and live our daily lives.
He who is pure and dwells on high —

May He inspire us to nobler living
And draw us close to Him.
May the battle-cry for all who seek freedom
Ever ring in our ears:
L'shono habo'o bi-Y'rusholoyim!
Next year in Jerusalem!

לְשָׁנָה
הַבָּאָה
בִּירוּשָׁלָיִם!

Jerusalem, which was established as the national capital of Judah by David, after he had consolidated and unified the nation, became, in time, more than just a political center. It became known as the City of God, and the Holy City (Isaiah 52). Thus, it exemplified all that was noble and sacred in Jewish life and Jewish thinking ever since.

The refrain, "Next Year in Jerusalem," which has been part of the Haggadah for many centuries, can best be understood as both an expression of the Jew's faith in the perfectibility of man, and in his constant, hopeful patience. This is a view widely shared by all freedom-loving people.

Alexis De Tocqueville expressed the first aspect of this concept well, when he wrote of America in his *Democracy in America,* ". . . they all consider society as a body in a state of improvement, humanity as a changing scene, in which nothing is, or ought to be, permanent; and they admit that what appears to them today to be good, may be superseded by something better tomorrow."

Henrik Ibsen, in *Peer Gynt,* gave expression to the second aspect of this concept when he wrote, "For fortune such as I've enjoyed, I have to thank America. My amply furnished library, I owe to Germany's later schools. From France, again, I get my waistcoats, my manners, and my spice of wit —from England, an industrious hand, and keen sense for my own advantage. The Jew has taught me how to wait."

פִּיּוּטִים וּזְמִירוֹת

Poems, Prayers and Hymns

We round out the Seder by reciting and chanting a number of poems, prayers and hymns that have, over the centuries, been appended to the main body of the Haggadah. These selections are filled with references and allusions drawn, primarily, from biblical law and lore. They summarize and emphasize, in beautiful poetic fashion, much of what we have expressed earlier in the evening.

In the Middle of the Night

This poem which carries as its refrain, "And it happened in the middle of the night," recalls many important events which, according to talmudic and midrashic interpretation, took place in the middle of the night. The poem concludes with an expression of faith in the coming of the Messiah, who will bring redemption. It was composed by the Palestinian poet, Yannai, in the seventh century.

Recite only on the first night of Passover:

וַיְהִי בַּחֲצִי הַלָּיְלָה

אָז רוֹב נִסִּים הִפְלֵאתָ בַּלַּיְלָה.   דַּנְתָּ מֶלֶךְ גְּרָר בַּחֲלוֹם הַלַּיְלָה.

בְּרֹאשׁ אַשְׁמוֹרוֹת זֶה הַלַּיְלָה.   הִפְחַדְתָּ אֲרַמִּי בְּאֶמֶשׁ לַיְלָה.

גֵּר צֶדֶק נִצַּחְתּוֹ כְּנֶחֱלַק לוֹ לַיְלָה.   וְיִשְׂרָאֵל יָשַׂר לָאֵל וַיּוּכַל לוֹ לַיְלָה.

וַיְהִי בַּחֲצִי הַלָּיְלָה.   וַיְהִי בַּחֲצִי הַלָּיְלָה.

זֶרַע בְּכוֹרֵי פַתְרוֹס מָחַצְתָּ בַּחֲצִי הַלָּיְלָה.
חֵילָם לֹא מָצְאוּ בְּקוּמָם בַּלָּיְלָה.
טִיסַת נְגִיד חֲרוֹשֶׁת סִלִּיתָ בְּכוֹכְבֵי לָיְלָה.
וַיְהִי בַּחֲצִי הַלָּיְלָה.

יָעַץ מְחָרֵף לְנוֹפֵף אִוּוּי הוֹבַשְׁתָּ פְּגָרָיו בַּלָּיְלָה.
כָּרַע בֵּל וּמַצָּבוֹ בְּאִישׁוֹן לָיְלָה.
לְאִישׁ חֲמוּדוֹת נִגְלָה רָז חֲזוֹת לָיְלָה.
וַיְהִי בַּחֲצִי הַלָּיְלָה.

מִשְׁתַּכֵּר בִּכְלֵי קֹדֶשׁ נֶהֱרַג בּוֹ בַּלָּיְלָה.
נוֹשַׁע מִבּוֹר אֲרָיוֹת פּוֹתֵר בִּעֲתוּתֵי לָיְלָה.
שִׂנְאָה נָטַר אֲגָגִי וְכָתַב סְפָרִים בַּלָּיְלָה.
וַיְהִי בַּחֲצִי הַלָּיְלָה.

עוֹרַרְתָּ נִצְחֲךָ עָלָיו בְּנֶדֶד שְׁנַת לָיְלָה.
פּוּרָה תִדְרוֹךְ לְשׁוֹמֵר מַה מִּלָּיְלָה.
צָרַח כַּשּׁוֹמֵר וְשָׂח אָתָא בֹקֶר וְגַם לָיְלָה.
וַיְהִי בַּחֲצִי הַלָּיְלָה.

קָרֵב יוֹם אֲשֶׁר הוּא לֹא יוֹם וְלֹא לָיְלָה.
רָם הוֹדַע כִּי לְךָ יוֹם אַף לְךָ הַלָּיְלָה.
שׁוֹמְרִים הַפְקֵד לְעִירְךָ כָּל הַיּוֹם וְכָל הַלָּיְלָה.
תָּאִיר כְּאוֹר יוֹם חֶשְׁכַּת לָיְלָה.
וַיְהִי בַּחֲצִי הַלָּיְלָה.

It is the Sacrifice of Passover

The liturgical poet, Elazar Ha-Kalir, a student of Yannai, composed this second supplementary hymn. There is a strong similarity in style, tone and content between the two poems. The refrain in this poem is, "And you shall say: 'It is a sacrifice of the Passover.'"

Recite only on the second night of Passover:

וַאֲמַרְתֶּם זֶבַח פֶּסַח

וּבְכֵן וַאֲמַרְתֶּם זֶבַח פֶּסַח.

אֹמֶץ גְּבוּרוֹתֶיךָ הִפְלֵאתָ בַּפֶּסַח. בְּרֹאשׁ כָּל מוֹעֲדוֹת נִשֵּׂאתָ פֶּסַח. גִּלִּיתָ לְאֶזְרָחִי חֲצוֹת לֵיל פֶּסַח.

וַאֲמַרְתֶּם זֶבַח פֶּסַח.

דְּלָתָיו דָּפַקְתָּ כְּחֹם הַיּוֹם בַּפֶּסַח. הִסְעִיד נוֹצְצִים עֻגוֹת מַצּוֹת בַּפֶּסַח. וְאֶל הַבָּקָר רָץ זֵכֶר לְשׁוֹר עֵרֶךְ פֶּסַח.

וַאֲמַרְתֶּם זֶבַח פֶּסַח.

זוֹעֲמוּ סְדוֹמִים וְלוֹהֲטוּ בָּאֵשׁ בַּפֶּסַח. חֻלַּץ לוֹט מֵהֶם וּמַצּוֹת אָפָה בְּקֵץ פֶּסַח. טֵאטֵאתָ אַדְמַת מוֹף וְנוֹף בְּעָבְרְךָ בַּפֶּסַח.

וַאֲמַרְתֶּם זֶבַח פֶּסַח.

יָה, רֹאשׁ כָּל אוֹן מָחַצְתָּ בְּלֵיל שִׁמּוּר
פֶּסַח. כַּבִּיר עַל בֵּן בְּכוֹר פָּסַחְתָּ בְּדַם פֶּסַח.
לְבִלְתִּי תֵּת מַשְׁחִית לָבֹא בִּפְתָחַי בַּפֶּסַח.
וַאֲמַרְתֶּם זֶבַח פֶּסַח.

מִסְגֶּרֶת סֻגְּרָה בְּעִתּוֹתֵי פֶּסַח. נִשְׁמְדָה
מִדְיָן בִּצְלִיל שְׂעוֹרֵי עֹמֶר פֶּסַח. שֹׂרְפוּ
מַשְׁמַנֵּי פוּל וְלוּד בִּיקַד יְקוֹד פֶּסַח.
וַאֲמַרְתֶּם זֶבַח פֶּסַח.

עוֹד הַיּוֹם בְּנוֹב לַעֲמוֹד עַד גָּעָה עוֹנַת
פֶּסַח. פַּס יָד כָּתְבָה לְקַעֲקֵעַ צוּל בַּפֶּסַח.
צָפֹה הַצָּפִית עָרוֹךְ הַשֻּׁלְחָן בַּפֶּסַח.
וַאֲמַרְתֶּם זֶבַח פֶּסַח.

קָהָל כִּנְּסָה הֲדַסָּה צוֹם לְשַׁלֵּשׁ בַּפֶּסַח.
רֹאשׁ מִבֵּית רָשָׁע מָחַצְתָּ בְּעֵץ חֲמִשִּׁים
בַּפֶּסַח. שְׁתֵּי אֵלֶּה רֶגַע תָּבִיא לְעוּצִית
בַּפֶּסַח. תָּעֹז יָדְךָ וְתָרוּם יְמִינְךָ כְּלֵיל
הִתְקַדֵּשׁ חַג פֶּסַח.

וַאֲמַרְתֶּם זֶבַח פֶּסַח.

104

All Praise Becomes Him

This attractive and lilting poem was composed in the Middle
Ages. Its author is unknown. The first letter of each of the key
Hebrew phrases follows the Hebrew alphabet from *alef* to *tuv*,
each emphasizing the Kingship of God. The alliterative refrain
ends with the words, "all praise becomes Him."

All read or sing in unison:

Refrain:

Lecho u-lecho,

Lecho kee lecho,

Lecho af lecho,

Lecho Adōnoy ha-mamlocho,

Kee lō na-eh,

Kee lō yo-eh.

כִּי לוֹ נָאֶה

אַדִּיר בִּמְלוּכָה. בָּחוּר כַּהֲלָכָה. גְּדוּדָיו
יֹאמְרוּ לוֹ. לְךָ וּלְךָ. לְךָ כִּי לְךָ. לְךָ אַף לְךָ.
לְךָ יְיָ הַמַּמְלָכָה. כִּי לוֹ נָאֶה. כִּי לוֹ יָאֶה.

דָּגוּל בִּמְלוּכָה. הָדוּר כַּהֲלָכָה. וָתִיקָיו
יֹאמְרוּ לוֹ. לְךָ וּלְךָ. לְךָ כִּי לְךָ. לְךָ אַף לְךָ.
לְךָ יְיָ הַמַּמְלָכָה. כִּי לוֹ נָאֶה. כִּי לוֹ יָאֶה.

זַכַּאי בִמְלוּכָה. חָסִין כַּהֲלָכָה. טַפְסְרָיו
יֹאמְרוּ לוֹ. לְךָ וּלְךָ. לְךָ כִּי לְךָ. לְךָ אַף לְךָ.
לְךָ יְיָ הַמַּמְלָכָה. כִּי לוֹ נָאֶה. כִּי לוֹ יָאֶה.

יָחִיד בִמְלוּכָה. כַּבִּיר כַּהֲלָכָה. לִמּוּדָיו
יֹאמְרוּ לוֹ. לְךָ וּלְךָ. לְךָ כִּי לְךָ. לְךָ אַף לְךָ.
לְךָ יְיָ הַמַּמְלָכָה. כִּי לוֹ נָאֶה. כִּי לוֹ יָאֶה.

מוֹשֵׁל בִמְלוּכָה. נוֹרָא כַּהֲלָכָה. סְבִיבָיו
יֹאמְרוּ לוֹ. לְךָ וּלְךָ. לְךָ כִּי לְךָ. לְךָ אַף לְךָ.
לְךָ יְיָ הַמַּמְלָכָה. כִּי לוֹ נָאֶה. כִּי לוֹ יָאֶה.

עָנָיו בִמְלוּכָה. פּוֹדֶה כַּהֲלָכָה. צַדִּיקָיו
יֹאמְרוּ לוֹ. לְךָ וּלְךָ. לְךָ כִּי לְךָ. לְךָ אַף לְךָ.
לְךָ יְיָ הַמַּמְלָכָה. כִּי לוֹ נָאֶה. כִּי לוֹ יָאֶה.

קָדוֹשׁ בִמְלוּכָה. רַחוּם כַּהֲלָכָה. שִׁנְאַנָּיו
יֹאמְרוּ לוֹ. לְךָ וּלְךָ. לְךָ כִּי לְךָ. לְךָ אַף לְךָ.
לְךָ יְיָ הַמַּמְלָכָה. כִּי לוֹ נָאֶה. כִּי לוֹ יָאֶה.

תַּקִּיף בִמְלוּכָה. תּוֹמֵךְ כַּהֲלָכָה. תְּמִימָיו
יֹאמְרוּ לוֹ. לְךָ וּלְךָ. לְךָ כִּי לְךָ. לְךָ אַף לְךָ.
לְךָ יְיָ הַמַּמְלָכָה. כִּי לוֹ נָאֶה. כִּי לוֹ יָאֶה.

All Praise Becomes Him

To be read responsively:

Majestic in sovereignty,
Deliberate in His ways,
His court sings to Him:
    "To Thee, yea to Thee,
    To Thee, and Thee alone,
    To Thee all sovereignty."
All praise becomes Him,
All praise becomes Him.

Pre-eminent in sovereignty,
Splendid in His ways,
His faithful sing to Him:
    "To Thee, yea to Thee,
    To Thee, and Thee alone,
    To Thee all sovereignty."
All praise becomes Him,
All praise becomes Him.

Pure in sovereignty,
Powerful in His ways,
His scribes sing to him:
    "To Thee, yea to Thee,
    To Thee, and Thee alone,
    To Thee all sovereignty."
All praise becomes Him,
All praise becomes Him.

One alone in sovereignty,
Mighty in His ways,
His disciples sing to Him:
    "To Thee, yea to Thee,
    To Thee, and Thee alone,
    To Thee all sovereignty."
All praise becomes Him,
All praise becomes Him.

Firm in His sovereignty,
Awesome in His ways,
His court sings to Him:
    "To Thee, yea to Thee,
    To Thee, and Thee alone,
    To Thee all sovereignty."
All praise becomes Him,
All praise becomes Him.

Humble in His sovereignty,
Redemptive in His ways,
His righteous ones sing to Him:
    "To Thee, yea to Thee,
    To Thee, and Thee alone,
    To Thee all sovereignty."
All praise becomes Him,
All praise becomes Him.

Holy in His sovereignty,
Merciful in His ways,
His hosts sing to Him:
    "To Thee, yea to Thee,
    To Thee, and Thee alone,
    To Thee all sovereignty."
All praise becomes Him,
All praise becomes Him.

Powerful in His sovereignty,
Sustaining in His ways,
His loyal ones sing to Him:
    "To Thee, yea to Thee,
    To Thee, and Thee alone,
    To Thee all sovereignty."
All praise becomes Him,
All praise becomes Him.

"There is no king who has not had a slave among his ancestors, and no slave who has not had a king among his."

HELEN KELLER

The Omer

The Book of Leviticus (chapter 23) prescribes that the first sheaf cut during the barley harvest was to be brought to the Temple as a sacrifice on the second day of Passover. It was forbidden to eat the new crop of grain until the *Omer* was sacrificed. Beginning with this second day of Passover, 49 days are counted, the 50th day being *Shavuos,* the Feast of Weeks. This period of counting is known as *Sefiro* (meaning, "counting"). Passover, the holiday of freedom, achieves its culmination on *Shavuos* when, according to tradition, the law (Torah) was given to the Israelites as they stood at the foot of Mount Sinai.

Recite on Second night of Passover:

בָּרוּךְ אַתָּה יְיָ אֱלֹהֵינוּ מֶלֶךְ הָעוֹלָם אֲשֶׁר קִדְּשָׁנוּ בְּמִצְוֹתָיו וְצִוָּנוּ עַל סְפִירַת הָעֹמֶר.

Boruch ato Adōnoy Elōhaynu melech ho-ōlom asher ki-d'shonu b'mitzvōsov v'tzeevonu al s'feeras ho-ōmer.

Praised be Thou, O Lord our God, King of the universe, Who has sanctified us with His commandments, and commanded us to count the Omer.

הַיּוֹם יוֹם אֶחָד לָעֹמֶר.

יְהִי רָצוֹן מִלְפָנֶיךָ יְיָ אֱלֹהֵינוּ וֵאלֹהֵי אֲבוֹתֵינוּ שֶׁיִּבָּנֶה בֵּית הַמִּקְדָּשׁ

בִּמְהֵרָה בְיָמֵינוּ וְתֵן חֶלְקֵנוּ בְּתוֹרָתֶךָ

109

אַדִּיר הוּא

God of Might, God of Right

This beautiful hymn, composed by an unknown author, was sung in France and Germany as early as the 15th century. Like the preceding poem, the Hebrew verses are composed in alphabetical acrostic form. The theme is one of adoration to God, and the Hebrew refrain, literally translated, is:

Speedily, speedily,
In our time, and soon,
May the Temple be rebuilt.

Adeer Hu Refrain:

Bi-m'hayro, bi-m'hayro,

B'yomaynu b'korōv,

Ayl b'nay, Ayl b'nay,

B'nay vayscho b'korōv.

God of might, God of right,
Thee we give all glory;
Thine all praise, in these days,
As in ages hoary;
When we hear, year by year,
Freedom's wondrous story.

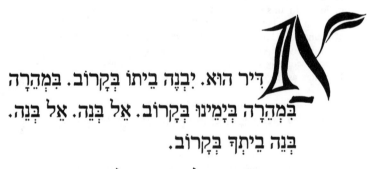

דִּיר הוּא. יִבְנֶה בֵּיתוֹ בְּקָרוֹב. בִּמְהֵרָה
בִּמְהֵרָה בְּיָמֵינוּ בְּקָרוֹב. אֵל בְּנֵה. אֵל בְּנֵה.
בְּנֵה בֵּיתְךָ בְּקָרוֹב.

בָּחוּר הוּא. גָּדוֹל הוּא. דָּגוּל הוּא. יִבְנֶה
בֵּיתוֹ בְּקָרוֹב. בִּמְהֵרָה בִּמְהֵרָה, בְּיָמֵינוּ
בְּקָרוֹב. אֵל בְּנֵה. אֵל בְּנֵה. בְּנֵה בֵּיתְךָ
בְּקָרוֹב.

אַדִּיר הוּא. וָתִיק הוּא. זַכַּאי הוּא. חָסִיד הוּא. יִבְנֶה בֵיתוֹ בְּקָרוֹב. בִּמְהֵרָה בִּמְהֵרָה בְּיָמֵינוּ בְּקָרוֹב. אֵל בְּנֵה. אֵל בְּנֵה. בְּנֵה בֵיתְךָ בְּקָרוֹב.

טָהוֹר הוּא. יָחִיד הוּא. כַּבִּיר הוּא. לָמוּד הוּא. מֶלֶךְ הוּא. נוֹרָא הוּא. סַגִּיב הוּא. עִזּוּז הוּא. פּוֹדֶה הוּא. צַדִּיק הוּא. יִבְנֶה בֵיתוֹ בְּקָרוֹב. בִּמְהֵרָה בִּמְהֵרָה, בְּיָמֵינוּ בְּקָרוֹב. אֵל בְּנֵה. אֵל בְּנֵה. בְּנֵה בֵיתְךָ בְּקָרוֹב.

קָדוֹשׁ הוּא. רַחוּם הוּא. שַׁדַּי הוּא. תַּקִּיף הוּא. יִבְנֶה בֵיתוֹ בְּקָרוֹב. בִּמְהֵרָה בִּמְהֵרָה, בְּיָמֵינוּ בְּקָרוֹב. אֵל בְּנֵה. אֵל בְּנֵה. בְּנֵה בֵיתְךָ בְּקָרוֹב.

אֶחָד מִי יוֹדֵעַ

Who Knows One?

This is an exciting numbers game in which the entire assembly can respond to each question, or each member can respond in turn. In content, it reviews every important event in the personal life of the Jew as it relates to his practice of Judaism. It also emphasizes the major precepts, concepts, and cultural institutions which are basic to Jewish life. The author of this poem is unknown, but probably dates back to the 15th or 16th centuries.

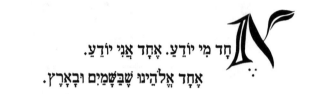

אֶחָד מִי יוֹדֵעַ. אֶחָד אֲנִי יוֹדֵעַ.
אֶחָד אֱלֹהֵינוּ שֶׁבַּשָּׁמַיִם וּבָאָרֶץ.

שְׁנַיִם מִי יוֹדֵעַ. שְׁנַיִם אֲנִי יוֹדֵעַ. שְׁנֵי לֻחוֹת הַבְּרִית. אֶחָד אֱלֹהֵינוּ שֶׁבַּשָּׁמַיִם וּבָאָרֶץ.

שְׁלֹשָׁה מִי יוֹדֵעַ. שְׁלֹשָׁה אֲנִי יוֹדֵעַ. שְׁלֹשָׁה אָבוֹת. שְׁנֵי לֻחוֹת הַבְּרִית. אֶחָד אֱלֹהֵינוּ שֶׁבַּשָּׁמַיִם וּבָאָרֶץ.

אַרְבַּע מִי יוֹדֵעַ. אַרְבַּע אֲנִי יוֹדֵעַ. אַרְבַּע אִמָּהוֹת. שְׁלֹשָׁה אָבוֹת. שְׁנֵי לֻחוֹת הַבְּרִית. אֶחָד אֱלֹהֵינוּ שֶׁבַּשָּׁמַיִם וּבָאָרֶץ.

חֲמִשָּׁה מִי יוֹדֵעַ. חֲמִשָּׁה אֲנִי יוֹדֵעַ. חֲמִשָּׁה חֻמְשֵׁי תוֹרָה. אַרְבַּע אִמָּהוֹת. שְׁלֹשָׁה אָבוֹת. שְׁנֵי לֻחוֹת הַבְּרִית. אֶחָד אֱלֹהֵינוּ שֶׁבַּשָּׁמַיִם וּבָאָרֶץ.

שִׁשָּׁה מִי יוֹדֵעַ. שִׁשָּׁה אֲנִי יוֹדֵעַ. שִׁשָּׁה סִדְרֵי מִשְׁנָה. חֲמִשָּׁה חֻמְשֵׁי תוֹרָה. אַרְבַּע אִמָּהוֹת. שְׁלֹשָׁה אָבוֹת. שְׁנֵי לֻחוֹת הַבְּרִית. אֶחָד אֱלֹהֵינוּ שֶׁבַּשָּׁמַיִם וּבָאָרֶץ.

שִׁבְעָה מִי יוֹדֵעַ. שִׁבְעָה אֲנִי יוֹדֵעַ. שִׁבְעָה יְמֵי שַׁבַּתָּא. שִׁשָּׁה סִדְרֵי מִשְׁנָה. חֲמִשָּׁה חֻמְשֵׁי תוֹרָה. אַרְבַּע אִמָּהוֹת. שְׁלשָׁה אָבוֹת. שְׁנֵי לֻחוֹת הַבְּרִית. אֶחָד אֱלֹהֵינוּ שֶׁבַּשָּׁמַיִם וּבָאָרֶץ.

שְׁמוֹנָה מִי יוֹדֵעַ. שְׁמוֹנָה אֲנִי יוֹדֵעַ. שְׁמוֹנָה יְמֵי מִילָה. שִׁבְעָה יְמֵי שַׁבַּתָּא. שִׁשָּׁה סִדְרֵי מִשְׁנָה. חֲמִשָּׁה חֻמְשֵׁי תוֹרָה. אַרְבַּע אִמָּהוֹת. שְׁלשָׁה אָבוֹת. שְׁנֵי לֻחוֹת הַבְּרִית. אֶחָד אֱלֹהֵינוּ שֶׁבַּשָּׁמַיִם וּבָאָרֶץ.

תִּשְׁעָה מִי יוֹדֵעַ. תִּשְׁעָה אֲנִי יוֹדֵעַ. תִּשְׁעָה יַרְחֵי לֵדָה. שְׁמוֹנָה יְמֵי מִילָה. שִׁבְעָה יְמֵי שַׁבַּתָּא. שִׁשָּׁה סִדְרֵי מִשְׁנָה. חֲמִשָּׁה חֻמְשֵׁי תוֹרָה. אַרְבַּע אִמָּהוֹת. שְׁלשָׁה אָבוֹת. שְׁנֵי לֻחוֹת הַבְּרִית. אֶחָד אֱלֹהֵינוּ שֶׁבַּשָּׁמַיִם וּבָאָרֶץ.

עֲשָׂרָה מִי יוֹדֵעַ. עֲשָׂרָה אֲנִי יוֹדֵעַ. עֲשָׂרָה דִבְּרַיָּא. תִּשְׁעָה יַרְחֵי לֵדָה. שְׁמוֹנָה יְמֵי מִילָה. שִׁבְעָה יְמֵי שַׁבַּתָּא. שִׁשָּׁה סִדְרֵי מִשְׁנָה. חֲמִשָּׁה חֻמְשֵׁי תוֹרָה. אַרְבַּע אִמָּהוֹת. שְׁלשָׁה אָבוֹת. שְׁנֵי לֻחוֹת הַבְּרִית. אֶחָד אֱלֹהֵינוּ שֶׁבַּשָּׁמַיִם וּבָאָרֶץ.

אַחַד עָשָׂר מִי יוֹדֵעַ. אַחַד עָשָׂר אֲנִי יוֹדֵעַ. אַחַד עָשָׂר כּוֹכְבַיָּא. עֲשָׂרָה דִבְּרַיָּא. תִּשְׁעָה יַרְחֵי לֵדָה. שְׁמוֹנָה יְמֵי מִילָה. שִׁבְעָה יְמֵי שַׁבַּתָּא. שִׁשָּׁה סִדְרֵי מִשְׁנָה. חֲמִשָּׁה חֻמְשֵׁי תוֹרָה. אַרְבַּע אִמָּהוֹת. שְׁלשָׁה אָבוֹת. שְׁנֵי לֻחוֹת הַבְּרִית. אֶחָד אֱלֹהֵינוּ שֶׁבַּשָּׁמַיִם וּבָאָרֶץ.

שְׁנֵים עָשָׂר מִי יוֹדֵעַ. שְׁנֵים עָשָׂר אֲנִי יוֹדֵעַ. שְׁנֵים עָשָׂר שִׁבְטַיָּא. אַחַד עָשָׂר כּוֹכְבַיָּא. עֲשָׂרָה דִבְּרַיָּא. תִּשְׁעָה יַרְחֵי לֵדָה. שְׁמוֹנָה יְמֵי מִילָה. שִׁבְעָה יְמֵי שַׁבַּתָּא. שִׁשָּׁה סִדְרֵי מִשְׁנָה. חֲמִשָּׁה חֻמְשֵׁי תוֹרָה. אַרְבַּע אִמָּהוֹת. שְׁלשָׁה אָבוֹת. שְׁנֵי לֻחוֹת הַבְּרִית. אֶחָד אֱלֹהֵינוּ שֶׁבַּשָּׁמַיִם וּבָאָרֶץ.

שְׁלשָׁה עָשָׂר מִי יוֹדֵעַ. שְׁלשָׁה עָשָׂר אֲנִי יוֹדֵעַ. שְׁלשָׁה עָשָׂר מִדַּיָּא. שְׁנֵים עָשָׂר שִׁבְטַיָּא. אַחַד עָשָׂר כּוֹכְבַיָּא. עֲשָׂרָה דִבְּרַיָּא. תִּשְׁעָה יַרְחֵי לֵדָה. שְׁמוֹנָה יְמֵי מִילָה. שִׁבְעָה יְמֵי שַׁבַּתָּא. שִׁשָּׁה סִדְרֵי מִשְׁנָה. חֲמִשָּׁה חֻמְשֵׁי תוֹרָה. אַרְבַּע אִמָּהוֹת. שְׁלשָׁה אָבוֹת. שְׁנֵי לֻחוֹת הַבְּרִית. אֶחָד אֱלֹהֵינוּ שֶׁבַּשָּׁמַיִם וּבָאָרֶץ.

Who Knows One?

Leader: ONE! Who knows One?

Assembly: I know One! One is our God, the God of the world.

Leader: TWO! Who knows Two?

Assembly: I know Two! Two are the tablets of stone. And One is our God, the God of the world.

Leader: THREE! Who knows Three?

Assembly: I know Three! Three are the patriarchs of Israel. Two are the tablets of stone. And One is our God, the God of the world.

Leader: FOUR! Who knows Four?

Assembly: I know Four! Four are the matriarchs of Israel. Three are the patriarchs. Two are the tablets. And One is our God, the God of the world.

Leader: FIVE! Who knows Five?

Assembly: I know Five! Five are the books of the Torah. Four are the matriarchs. Three are the patriarchs. Two are the tablets. And One is our God, the God of the world.

Leader: SIX! Who knows Six?

Assembly: I know Six! Six sections of the Mishna. Five books of the Torah. Four matriarchs. Three patriarchs. Two tablets. And One is our God, the God of the world.

Leader:	SEVEN! Who knows Seven?
Assembly:	I know Seven! Seven are the days of the week. Six sections of the Mishna. Five books of the Torah. Four matriarchs. Three patriarchs. Two tablets. And One is our God, the God of the world.
Leader:	EIGHT! Who knows Eight?
Assembly:	I know eight! Eight days of initiation.[1] Seven days of the week. Six sections of Mishna. Five books of Torah. Four matriarchs. Three patriarchs. Two tablets. And One is our God, the God of the world.
Leader:	NINE! Who knows Nine?
Assembly:	I know Nine! Nine months for childbirth. Eight days of initiation. Seven days of the week. Six sections of Mishna. Five books of Torah. Four matriarchs. Three patriarchs. Two tablets. And One is our God, the God of the world.
Leader:	TEN! Who knows Ten?
Assembly:	I know Ten! Ten are the commandments. Nine months of childbirth. Eight days of initiation. Seven days of the week. Six sections of Mishna. Five books of Torah. Four matriarchs. Three patriarchs. Two tablets. And One is our God, the God of the world.
Leader:	ELEVEN! Who knows Eleven?
Assembly:	I know Eleven! Eleven are the stars. Ten are the commandments. Nine months of childbirth. Eight days of initiation. Seven days of the week. Six sections of Mishna. Five books of Torah. Four matriarchs. Three patriarchs. Two tablets. And One is our God, the God of the world.

---

[1] The "covenant of circumcision," also referred to as "the covenant of Abraham, is performed on the eighth day after the birth of a boy. It marks his initiation into the Jewish fold.

Leader: TWELVE! Who knows Twelve?

Assembly: I know Twelve! Twelve are the tribes. Eleven are the stars. Ten are the commandments. Nine months of childbirth. Eight days of initiation. Seven days of the week. Six sections of Mishna. Five books of Torah. Four matriarchs. Three patriarchs. Two tablets. And One is our God, the God of the world.

Leader: THIRTEEN! Who knows Thirteen?

Assembly: I know Thirteen! Thirteen are the attributes of God. Twelve are the tribes. Eleven are the stars. Ten are the commandments. Nine months of childbirth. Eight days of initiation. Seven days of the week. Six sections of Mishna. Five books of Torah. Four matriarchs. Three patriarchs. Two tablets. One is our God, the God of the world.

One Only Kid

חַד גַּדְיָא

In this beautiful folktale, the story of the Jewish people is retold. A father bought a little goat for two *zuzim,* two small coins. And then a cat came along and devoured the goat; a dog came along and bit the cat; a stick came along and beat the dog, etc. So it was with the Jewish people. One nation after the other inflicted punishment upon Israel and conquered it, but only for a while. The tale ends with the message that in the end God conquers all and sets justice aright.

"The use of force alone is but *temporary*. It may subdue for a moment, but it does not remove the necessity of subduing again; and a nation is not governed, which is perpetually to be conquered."

EDMUND BURKE

117

ד גַּדְיָא חַד גַּדְיָא דְזַבָּן אַבָּא בִּתְרֵי זוּזֵי.

חַד גַּדְיָא חַד גַּדְיָא.

וְאָתָא שׁוּנְרָא. וְאָכְלָה לְגַדְיָא. דְזַבָּן אַבָּא בִּתְרֵי זוּזֵי.

חַד גַּדְיָא חַד גַּדְיָא.

וְאָתָא כַלְבָּא. וְנָשַׁךְ לְשׁוּנְרָא. דְּאָכְלָה לְגַדְיָא. דְזַבָּן אַבָּא בִּתְרֵי זוּזֵי.

חַד גַּדְיָא חַד גַּדְיָא.

וְאָתָא חוּטְרָא. וְהִכָּה לְכַלְבָּא. דְּנָשַׁךְ לְשׁוּנְרָא. דְּאָכְלָה לְגַדְיָא. דְזַבָּן אַבָּא בִּתְרֵי זוּזֵי.

חַד גַּדְיָא חַד גַּדְיָא.

וְאָתָא נוּרָא. וְשָׂרַף לְחוּטְרָא. דְהִכָּה לְכַלְבָּא. דְּנָשַׁךְ לְשׁוּנְרָא. דְּאָכְלָה לְגַדְיָא. דְזַבָּן אַבָּא בִּתְרֵי זוּזֵי.

חַד גַּדְיָא חַד גַּדְיָא.

וְאָתָא מַיָא. וְכָבָה לְנוּרָא. דְשָׂרַף לְחוּטְרָא. דְהִכָּה לְכַלְבָּא. דְּנָשַׁךְ לְשׁוּנְרָא. דְּאָכְלָה לְגַדְיָא. דְזַבָּן אַבָּא בִּתְרֵי זוּזֵי.

חַד גַּדְיָא חַד גַּדְיָא.

וְאָתָא תוֹרָא. וְשָׁתָא לְמַיָא. דְּכָבָה לְנוּרָא. דְשָׂרַף לְחוּטְרָא. דְהִכָּה לְכַלְבָּא. דְּנָשַׁךְ לְשׁוּנְרָא. דְּאָכְלָה לְגַדְיָא. דְזַבָּן אַבָּא בִּתְרֵי זוּזֵי.

חַד גַּדְיָא חַד גַּדְיָא.

וְאָתָא הַשּׁוֹחֵט. וְשָׁחַט לְתוֹרָא. דְּשָׁתָא לְמַיָּא. דְּכָבָה לְנוּרָא. דְּשָׂרַף לְחוּטְרָא. דְּהִכָּה לְכַלְבָּא. דְּנָשַׁךְ לְשׁוּנְרָא. דְּאָכְלָה לְגַדְיָא. דְּזַבֵּן אַבָּא בִּתְרֵי זוּזֵי.

חַד גַּדְיָא חַד גַּדְיָא.

וְאָתָא מַלְאַךְ הַמָּוֶת. וְשָׁחַט לְשׁוֹחֵט. דְּשָׁחַט לְתוֹרָא. דְּשָׁתָא לְמַיָּא. דְּכָבָה לְנוּרָא. דְּשָׂרַף לְחוּטְרָא. דְּהִכָּה לְכַלְבָּא. דְּנָשַׁךְ לְשׁוּנְרָא. דְּאָכְלָה לְגַדְיָא. דְּזַבֵּן אַבָּא בִּתְרֵי זוּזֵי.

חַד גַּדְיָא חַד גַּדְיָא.

וְאָתָא הַקָּדוֹשׁ בָּרוּךְ הוּא. וְשָׁחַט לְמַלְאַךְ הַמָּוֶת. דְּשָׁחַט לְשׁוֹחֵט. דְּשָׁחַט לְתוֹרָא. דְּשָׁתָא לְמַיָּא. דְּכָבָה לְנוּרָא. דְּשָׂרַף לְחוּטְרָא. דְּהִכָּה לְכַלְבָּא. דְּנָשַׁךְ לְשׁוּנְרָא. דְּאָכְלָה לְגַדְיָא. דְּזַבֵּן אַבָּא בִּתְרֵי זוּזֵי.

חַד גַּדְיָא חַד גַּדְיָא.

One Only Kid

One only kid!
One only kid!
That father bought
For two zuzim.
One only kid; one only kid.

Then came the cat
And ate the kid,
That father bought
For two zuzim.
One only kid; one only kid.

Then came the dog
And bit the cat,
That ate the kid,
That father bought
For two zuzim.
One only kid; one only kid.

Then came the stick
And beat the dog,
That bit the cat,
That ate the kid,
That father bought
For two zuzim.
One only kid; one only kid.

Then came the fire
And burned the stick,
That beat the dog,
That bit the cat,
That ate the kid,
That father bought
For two zuzim.
One only kid; one only kid.

Then came the water
And quenched the fire,
That burned the stick,
That beat the dog,
That bit the cat,
That ate the kid,
That father bought
For two zuzim.
One only kid; one only kid.

Then came the ox
And drank the water,
That quenched the fire,
That burned the stick,

That beat the dog,
That bit the cat,
That ate the kid,
That father bought
For two zuzim.
One only kid; one only kid.

Then came the slaughterer
And slaughtered the ox,
That drank the water,
That quenched the fire,
That burned the stick,
That beat the dog,
That bit the cat,
That ate the kid,
That father bought
For two zuzim.
One only kid; one only kid.

Then came death's angel
And slew the slaughterer,
That slaughtered the ox,
That drank the water,
That quenched the fire,
That burned the stick,
That beat the dog,
That bit the cat,
That ate the kid,
That father bought
For two zuzim.
One only kid; one only kid.

Then came the Holy One,
    Blessed be He,
And destroyed death's angel,
That slew the slaughterer,
That slaughtered the ox,
That drank the water,

That quenched the fire,
That burned the stick,
That beat the dog,
That bit the cat,
That ate the kid,
That father bought
For two zuzim.
One only kid; one only kid.

The Seder Is Over

Quite appropriately, the Haggadah ends on a note of triumph. Truth, justice and lovingkindness are the nemeses of slavery, tyranny and oppression.

The weak may be overcome by the strong, but only for a while, for there are always new, emerging forces, that crush the seemingly invincible forces prevailing for the moment.

Rabbi Judah bar Ilai, a disciple of Rabbi Akiba, witnessed the martyrdom of his beloved teacher at the hands of the Romans, and then made the following poignant, and eternally valid observation:

> Rock is strong,
> But iron shatters it.
> Fire melts iron;
> Water extinguishes fire;
> Clouds carry away water,
> And wind drives away clouds;
> Man can withstand the wind,
> But fear conquers man;
> Wine dispels fear,
> But sleep overcomes wine.
> And death rules over sleep.
>
> But, more powerful than all ten,
> Are sweet acts of charity and lovingkindness.

This is the power of Passover. This is the lesson of history. Twenty-five centuries ago, the prophet Zechariah stated it well for men of all ages and lands. To his demoralized and despondent fellow-Jews, who were trying to rebuild their destroyed Temple and their despoiled land, he said:

"Not by might, nor by power," saith the Lord,
"but by My spirit."

This is God operating in history. This is the story of freedom.